A PASSION FOR *Prayer*

Books by Timothy E. Crosby and Lonnie Melashenko

In the Presence of Angels (Pacific Press)
A Passion for Prayer

To order, call **1-800-765-6955.**
    Visit us at www.rhpa.org for information on other Review and Herald products.

FINDING A NEW
AND DEEPER
INTIMACY
WITH GOD

A PASSION FOR Prayer

Tim Crosby ✦ Ruthie Jacobsen ✦ Lonnie Melashenko

REVIEW AND HERALD® PUBLISHING ASSOCIATION
HAGERSTOWN, MD 21740

This book was
Edited by Gerald Wheeler
Copyedited by Bill Cleveland and James Cavil
Designed by GenesisDesign
Cover photos by PhotoDisc
Typeset: 12/14 Stone Serif

PRINTED IN U.S.A.

02 01 00 99 98   5 4 3 2

R&H Cataloging Service
Crosby, Timothy Eugene, 1954-
    Passion for prayer: finding a new and deeper
intimacy with God, by Tim Crosby, Ruthie Jacobsen, and
Lonnie Melashenko.

    1. Prayer.   I. Jacobsen, Ruth, joint author.   II. Melashenko,
E. Lonnie, 1947-   , joint author.   III. Title.

                    242

ISBN 0-8280-1355-1

Contents

CHAPTER 1

In the Beginning God

Please come with us on a mind's-eye tour of a lovely rest home. In the main room we see a dignified, white-haired man sitting alone. He's clearly lonely. The nurses attend to his every need, but no one is fellowshipping with him. We learn that he is, in fact, the founder of the rest home and that he has many children, but they rarely ever visit him. Occasionally they call, but they don't talk long. No one touches him.

Do you know who this old man is?

He's God.

Do you think God ever feels like that? He created the world, gives us life, salvation, and so many lesser delights, but so few of His children ever thank Him or remember Him. Oh, yes, choirs of attending angels surround Him, but still, He must get lonely for His estranged human children who spend so little time fellowshipping with Him.

Now let's change the picture. Picture this white-haired gentleman with a cat on his lap. He's stroking the cat, which purrs and rubs its head against his hand. Now the man is not lonely anymore. He's found a friend. Although the furry, purry creature cannot meet his intellectual needs, it meets his emotional need for love and affection. And you can be sure that the cat gets the very best food and care from its friend.

God longs to fellowship with His children, the sheep of His pasture, just as you and I love to spend time with our pets.

When Tim and Carol Crosby lived in California, they owned two purebred Persians, Sir Barnum Tugglesby and Sir Bailey Snugglefluff. Barnum and Bailey were beautiful to behold. But they were handicapped in the affection department. About the only time they rubbed up against a leg was when their food bowl was empty. Tim and Carol were never happy with these cats. They were disappointed that the only time the animals wanted to be around them was when they wanted something; disappointed that these cats that were bought at such great price showed so little affection.

Does God feel that way about you?

But now the Crosbys have Beaupouff, a pure white longhair. Although Beaupouff lacks the pedigree of the former purebreds, she's more affectionate. And that makes it worth all the kitty litter.

What does God want from us first and foremost? Well, what does a parent want from a child, or a pet owner from a pet? Perfection? Service? No. Love. What God wants from us, first and foremost, is our companionship, our affection. Sometimes God must feel like the proverbial lonely wife whose husband is always off making money but never has time for his bride. God wants us to spend time with Him before we work hard for Him. *He wants us to purr in His lap.*

Maybe you're not a cat lover. OK, let's talk about dogs. Do you know that our word canine is related to the Greek word for worship? The Greek word for worship is *proskuneo*, and from that root we get our word canine. Now, what would worship have to do with a dog?

Think about it. You have probably experienced firsthand a dog's adulation. A dog that is happy to see you will prance around in a sort of dance of celebration, wagging its tail, rejoicing in your presence and doing all it can to say in doggy language that you are someone special. The animal may even jump up on you, trying to get as close as possible, seeking your face. That's worship. Leaping before the Lord. Purring in His lap. Snuggling up. Seeking His face. We could learn something from our pets.

Going off to battle the day without giving God so much as a nod is not merely inadvisable, it's unnatural. Mitzi, the Crosbys' former toy poodle, was never taught religion. But upon being released from her cage in the morning, she would instinctively come to greet her master before she ever went to play with her toys, or even before she went outside to tend to the call of nature.

As we said, we could learn something. . . .

～

The first words of Scripture are "In the beginning God." That is a recipe for spiritual success.

God, in the beginning, took chaos and turned it into a garden. It is encouraging to know that this sorry mess of sin that we find ourselves in is going to end right, because it began right—even if it went wrong somewhere in the middle.

"In the beginning God" is a great life motto. We seek God at the beginning of every day so that He can regenerate the deep currents of our souls by the same creative power that made the seas and all that in them is. Just as the Spirit of God moved upon the face of the deep and began to rearrange and organize the primordial chaos, bringing order and abundance, so the Spirit of God moves upon the deep recesses of the heart in the morning when we present ourselves to Him, making us fruitful. In the morning, while the heart is fresh and pliable, we push away the cares of the day and throw open the door of communion with God and drink our fill of Him.

Finding time for a consistent prayer life is never easy. It wasn't easy for Jesus, either. Luke 5:16 says that Jesus often withdrew to lonely places and prayed. According to Mark 1:35 His practice was to rise early, in the very beginning of the day, and go to a secluded place to pray, setting the currents of His life flowing in the right direction. It was only because He withdrew from the crowds that Jesus was able to draw the crowds.

Now we tend to think that since Jesus lived in a simpler age—no 9:00-to-5:00 job, no television, no housework—finding time for prayer must have been easy. Oh? Let's take a look at a typical day in His life and observe the hurdles He had to overcome before He could find time to pray. Sometimes getting up before the sun didn't work, because the people would follow Him (Luke 4:42). So once He went on a retreat. Or tried to.

Herod had recently beheaded John the Baptist. Jesus felt the need for meditation and prayer. Matthew tells us that "when Jesus heard what had happened, he withdrew by boat privately to a solitary place." But somehow there was a security leak, and the news got out. "Hearing of this, the crowds followed him on foot from the towns. When Jesus landed and saw a large crowd, he had compassion on them and healed their sick" (Matt. 14:13, 14).

Jesus had not planned on 5,000 people tagging along with Him on His retreat. His life, like ours, was full of interruptions. In fact, some of Jesus' greatest works were reactions to interruptions. Jesus had to set aside His plans to help people out of a jam they had gotten themselves into by poor planning. He was not a cook, but He had to postpone His prayer life to feed 5,000 people. Think about it: the feeding of the 5,000 was an interruption! Remember that the next time your plans are interrupted by someone in need.

Finally it was time to send the people home. "Immediately Jesus made the disciples get into the boat and go on ahead of him to the other side, while he dismissed the crowd. After he had dismissed them, he went up on a mountainside by himself to pray. When evening came, he was there alone" (verses 22, 23).

Ahhhh! Alone at last! Finally Jesus could pour out His heart to His Father. He had several hours to Himself before duty called once more. Actually, it was 12 seasoned seamen scared out of their wits by a seasonal storm on Galilee that summoned Him. And over the howling wind and across the miles, Jesus heard their cry. The Son of God, who had battled sleep after a long day of ministry to approach His Father, now headed for the storm-battered boat of disciples on the water and calmed their fears.

Only those who have wrestled with God can calmly walk on the storm.

Somehow Jesus found time to pray, even if he had to stay up all night to do it. And today most of us have a lot more time for prayer than Jesus did, because we don't have crowds of people following us around and hanging on our every word.

~

Perhaps one reason we don't have a desire to spend time with God, as Jesus did, is that we don't know how to pray rightly to allow Him to evoke within our hearts a wellspring of joy. Prayer is a burden because it is not communion with a lover. Instead, it's more like dictation to a secretary. "Do this, that, and the other thing—and by 5:00 please."

We can gauge our spiritual maturity to some extent by the content of our prayers. Immature Christians spend most of their prayer time on their personal wish list. "Give me this;" "Help me do that." God is their shield and *butler*. They tell God what they want Him to do, and He carries out their wishes.

But not always. Which makes Him a rather poor butler.

Mature Christians also ask for personal favors, but that does not occupy the majority of their prayer time. The prayers of a mature Christian tend to include much more praise and thanksgiving to God and intercession for others, because they understand a secret, first expressed by David Yonggi Cho:

When we meet God's needs, He will meet ours.

Here is one of the most profound principles of Christian life. At first it sounds almost blasphemous. God doesn't have any needs—does He? What needs could God possibly have that we could fill?

Have you ever noticed the first three words and the last

three words in Ellen White's five-volume Conflict of the Ages Series? The first three words in the book *Patriarchs and Prophets* and the last three words in the book *The Great Controversy* are "God is love."

Now, love has an infinite capacity for companionship and fellowship. In *The Desire of Ages* we find the following statement: "Our Redeemer thirsts for recognition. He hungers for the sympathy and love of those whom He has purchased with His own blood. He longs with inexpressible desire that they should come to Him and have life" (p. 191).

God is thirsty for your companionship. You see, you have a unique experience with Him—a unique testimony. You can understand Him in a particular way that nobody else can. He has bestowed upon each one of us a distinctive gift of His grace. He longs to reveal in you a unique part of His character. He has needs that only the special configuration of your heart can supply. God yearns for the pleasure of your company.

The Lord has already provided everything we will ever need, not only for our salvation but also for our happiness. He purchased our eternity by His blood on the cross. Now all He wants in return is our love. He endured the shame for the joy that lay ahead of Him (Heb. 12:2). You are part of that joy. Our prayers are like incense—perfume—to God (Ps. 141:2; Rev. 5:8). They make His life sweeter.

If you want to see God's miracle-working power in your life, then learn to spend time adoring Him. Lay your wish list aside for a while and simply "purr" in His presence. Tell Him that you are nothing without Him. Claim the promise He made to Abram in Genesis 15:1: "I am your shield, your very great reward." Tell Him that He is the only reward you want, that your supreme desire is to bask in the smile of His face. Confess your inability to love Him as He loves you and ask Him to place within you a hunger, a yearning for Him. Seek his Spirit. Tell Him in detail how much you appreciate all that He has done for you and how little you understand it. Ask Him to teach you how to praise Him, to give you the attitude of praise.

If you *don't* love Him, if you *don't* appreciate how much

He has done, then tell Him how much you *want* to love and appreciate Him. That's good enough. God accepts that. And when you put God first and meet His needs, He'll take care of yours, because *God always gives better than He gets.*

~

Fellowship with the King of kings is the peak experience in the universe. It is the ultimate reward. And we can begin to enjoy it now.

We fallen creatures, with damaged hearts, let our love for God get crowded out by earthly things. But if we ask God to give us a yearning for Him, an appetite for Him, He will do it. God has given us this promise: "Delight yourself in the Lord and he will give you the desires of your heart" (Ps. 37:4). As your experience with God matures, your understanding of this passage may change. At first you may think of it this way: If you delight yourself in the Lord, then He will give you the things you really want. God will seem to be a means to an end. But more and more you will discover that all you really want is God.

A lot of wonderful things happen to people who pray. But the most wonderful outcome is that we are drawn into spiritual intimacy with God. And intimacy with God is the ultimate reward. It's the best possible thing in the universe. Little children think that the greatest reward is a candy bar. But it isn't. Grown-ups assume the ultimate reward is power or wealth or prestige or security or romance. But it isn't. The ultimate reward is intimacy with God.

In Michael H. Macdonald and Andrew A. Tadie's *G. K Chesterton and C. S. Lewis: The Riddle of Joy*, Peter J. Kreeft cites Augustine's thought experiment in his sermon "On the Pure Love of God." Imagine, says Augustine, that God appeared to you and said He would make a deal with you, that He would give you everything you wished, everything your heart desired, except one thing. You could have anything you imagine; nothing would be impossible for you, and nothing would be sinful or forbidden. But, God concluded, "you shall never see My face."

Why, Augustine asks, did a terrible chill creep over your heart at those last words unless there is in your heart a love of God, a desire for Him? In fact, if you wouldn't accept that deal, you really love God above all things, for look what you just did: you gave up the whole world, and more, for God.

One of the authors of this volume stumbled onto this statement on June 30, 1995, and wrote this in their journal: "It has been only a few hours since I first read this. I am still stunned by my emotional reaction to it. As soon as I began to consider the question, the word 'no!' sprang impulsively to mind, then an overwhelming sorrow. 'Never, never, never,' I sobbed, over and over again. I was imagining the loss of the ultimate dream. It was a while before I could recollect myself, but the end result was a gentle joy."

God invites us through the prophet Jeremiah to an intimate prayer relationship with him. "'I know the plans I have for you,' declares the Lord, 'plans to prosper you and not to harm you, plans to give you hope and a future. Then you will call upon me and come and pray to me, and I will listen to you. You will seek me and find me when you seek me with all your heart'" (Jer. 29:11-13).

And in Jeremiah 33:3 He says, "Call to me and I will answer you and tell you great and unsearchable things you do not know." God has a lot to offer to those who seek Him.

Fellowship with God is a wonderful experience. We're not talking about a special holier-than-thouness, but an abiding joy. We're not talking about making God our slap-happy "buddy." We approach the throne of grace boldly (Heb 4:16), but with humility, awe, and wonder. Intimacy has to be cultivated—it doesn't come in an instant. But once you have it, nothing else in the world can compare with it.

How do you get it? It comes through ministry to others and through prayer. Why not get serious about prayer today? Just don't overdo it at first. You would not begin an exercise regimen by attempting to run a marathon, so don't start out by trying to pray an hour a day. Start with 10 minutes and increase it one minute each week. Choose a set place and time of day, then discipline yourself over a period of months. If you can't concentrate while kneeling, then pray while walking. Whenever you are alone, pray out loud. This aids in concentration, and the prayer tends to have more impact, at least on the one praying. Keep a notepad in your pocket to write down things that come to your mind (prayer inspires creativity) so that you can then put them out of your mind and continue praying. Pretty soon you'll be looking forward to your time with God. First, your prayers will change you, and then you can start working on changing your world.

Oh, it takes time. When you begin to map out substantial time with the Lord, at first you may have to drag those recalcitrant emotions, kicking and screaming, into order. And it may not be easy the first time, or the second, or even the third. At least that was Oswald Chambers' experience when he first began, all at once, to devote an hour a day to prayer.

Every so often one of the emotions would jump up and scream, "I don't want to be here," and go running off on some daydream, and Chambers would have to grab them by the tail and bring them back. At first it was all hard work.

But as every psychologist knows, the most effective way to change our feelings is to change our behaviour. If you keep at it, you, like Chambers, will find that soon those emotions will quiet down, because they realize you're in charge. They may grumble now and then, but they know they have to go along.

Then suddenly one glorious day, after a month or two of disciplined prayer, one of the most obstreperous of those emotions will jump right up and say, "Glory," and another one will shout, "Hallelujah!" Your entire being will be happily coordinated in the practice of prayer. And you will discover the joy of intimacy with God.

Perhaps you feel a gentle tug on your heart just now to kneel down and talk to Him, or maybe just to slip outside in the dark and walk through the garden or down the lane and share your deepest secrets with Him. That little voice you hear is God knocking on the door of your heart and saying, "Can you come out and pray with Me? I'll make it worth your while."

~

If the ultimate desire of your heart is for Him, who knows what might happen to you? Sometimes God surprises those who seek Him by ambushing them with grace—even when they're just going through the motions.

Consider what happened to Brennan Manning. He had broken up with his girlfriend Barbara to enter a monastery. His brother made a $50 bet with him that he wouldn't last a week. Sure enough, Brennan discovered that he wasn't cut out for the spiritual life. His account of what happened next is one of the most moving in contemporary Christian literature. The experience eventually led Manning out of the priesthood. He got married and today is a popular speaker at retreats and revivals around the country. But the point is that Jesus can meet us anywhere.

"After seven days," he writes, "I decided to pack it in. They were going to kick me out anyway. I'd lasted the week, so I could collect the $50 from my brother. I hoped Barbara would still be drying her tears. I could commend her for her patience and undying love, we would be reconciled, I would return to Missouri, and we'd be married in June. A narrow escape from my flirtation with death.

"I packed my suitcase and went to Father Augustine's office to inform him of my departure. He wasn't there. I decided to stop into the chapel and say goodbye to God. 'Thank You, God (this is Richie), for showing me that the priesthood is not my calling. Please have Barbara waiting when I get back to Brooklyn. As a sign of my good-will, I'll go to Mass one extra time a week for a whole year. [I thought that would impress Him that He wasn't dealing with some shallow soul.] Well, goodbye, God. I'll catch You in Brooklyn.'

"I returned to the seat of power but Augustine still had not arrived. Never one to shun the heroic, I decided to go back to the chapel and do something great for God. Even though it wasn't required, I would visit each of the fourteen 'stations of the Cross.' I grabbed a book and followed the directions. At the first station, 'Jesus is condemned to death,' I read the prayer, made a hasty genuflection like I'd smelled smoke in the building, and hurried on to the second one. *Maybe when I'm working for The New Yorker, I thought, I'll rewrite these archaic prayers, put them in modern idiom, and do the Church a favor. Maybe the Pope will make me a knight of St. Gregory or something.*

"After eleven minutes of praying and genuflecting, I checked into the twelfth station, 'Jesus died on the Cross.' The rubric in the book said, 'kneel.' As I sank to my knees, the Angelus bell from the cloistered Carmelite monastery three miles away sounded in the distance. It was noon.

"At five minutes after *three,* I rose from my knees, and went in search of a Bible. I had never read the Bible before but knew that I had to read the Gospels. I couldn't find one in the monastery. In those days, it was considered a Protestant book.

"During those three hours on my knees I felt like a little boy kneeling at the seashore. Little waves washed up and lapped at my knees. Slowly the waves grew bigger and stronger till they reached my waist. Suddenly a tremendous wave of concussion force knocked me over backward and swept me off the beach reeling in midair, arching through space, vaguely aware that I was being carried to a place I had never been before—the heart of Jesus Christ. When He called my name, it was not Richie or Brennan, but another word that I shall not disclose, a word that is my very own name, spoken with infinite love. It is the sweetest sound I shall ever hear, the name by which Jesus knows me. It must be what Mary Magdalene responded to when Jesus in the garden said simply, 'Mary'—except that in my case He did not call me by my given name.

"In this first-ever-in-my-life experience of being unconditionally loved, I moved back and forth between mild ecstasy and hushed trembling. The aura was what George Maloney years later would describe as 'bright darkness.' And bewildering strength. The moment lingered on and on in a timeless now until without warning I felt a hand grip my heart. I could barely breathe. It was abrupt and startling. The awareness of being loved was no longer gentle, tender and comfortable. The love of Christ, the crucified Son of God, for me, took on the wildness, passion, and fury of a sudden spring storm. Like a bursting dam, spasms of convulsive crying erupted from the depths of my being. He died on the Cross for me! I had known that before, but in the way that Cardinal Newman describes as notional knowledge—abstract, far away, largely irrelevant to the gut issues of life, just another trinket in the dusty pawnshop of dogmatic beliefs. But in one blinding moment of salvific truth, it was real knowledge calling for personal engagement of my mind and heart. Christianity was no longer simply a moral code but a love affair, the thrill, the excitement, the incredible passionate joy of being loved and falling in love with Jesus Christ.

"At last, drained, spent, feeling limp and lost in speechless humility, I was back kneeling at the seashore with quiet, calm waves of love sweeping over me like a gentle tide saturating my mind and heart in a tranquil mode of deepest worship.

"When at 3:05 p.m. I rose shakily from the floor, glanced at my watch in disbelief, resonated with awe and wonder and, unable to find a Bible, returned to my cell and unpacked my bag, I knew that the most thrilling adventure of my life had just begun. It was a new mode of existence and Paul describes it well in Colossians 3:11 (Jerusalem): 'There is only Christ: he is everything'" (Brennan Manning, *Lion and Lamb: The Relentless Tenderness of Jesus* [Chosen Books, 1986]).

Jesus is calling you into intimate fellowship with Him. Seek His face with all your heart, and you will find that special place reserved for you deep in the heart of God.

CHAPTER 2

Asking for Great Things

Suppose that an official-looking letter arrived at your home one day with your name typed (not laser-printed) on the front of the envelope. Opening the letter, you glance at the letterhead, and it says very simply: The White House. Inside is a personal letter from the president of the United States inviting you to give him a telephone call on a given date and time to share with the national leader some suggestions of things you would like to see changed. "I will take your call in person," said the writer. "I'll make it worth your while." At the bottom of the letter is the signature of the president. It does not appear to be machine written.

You say, "Honey, look at this! What do you think of it?"

Your spouse reads the letter, then says, "Yeah, right. And I bet he has a bridge in Brooklyn to sell you."

"Well, it looks real," you reply. "I'm gonna check it out." You dial the White House number given in the letter to find out if it's true.

A pleasant female voice answers: "This is the White House."

You say, "Uh, this is ———, and I want to confirm that this invitation from the president I'm holding in my hand is for real."

"Well, may I ask what it says?"

You tell her.

She replies, "Just a moment, please. Let me look up your name."

A minute later she's back. She addresses you respectfully by name and says, "That invitation is for real. The president will be expecting your call this Thursday at 10:00 p.m."

So you say (now get this): "Well, I'm sorry, but I doubt if I'll have time to talk to the president. I've got a favorite TV program that comes on about then, and I really want to watch it, so please tell him thanks anyway."

What's wrong with this story? You ought to be excited out of your socks! Who would pass up an opportunity like that?

Yet we pass up even greater opportunities every day. Each of us has an open invitation for a private talk with the President of the universe. We are free to talk as long as we want to the One at the center of power; we have unlimited access to His throne. We can choose to become part of God's inner circle. And history has proven that we can trust Him to hear and answer.

Why do we neglect to take advantage of this most amazing opportunity ever offered to human beings? When life throws bricks at us, we don't have to take it lying down. We've got friends in high places!

Lonnie's job as *Voice of Prophecy* speaker comes with a rewarding perk: he gets to read the mail whenever he wants. Some of those incredible letters are heartwarming; others are heart-wrenching and tragic, written by people who have problems piled on top of problems. But now and then there is a rather humorous letter, such as this one:

"The Lord is so good to me, and I don't deserve it. A few years ago I had a lot of trouble getting my Social Security check. They said, 'We sent it,' so I blamed the post office. So the same old story kept on. I called our congressman. They tried, but still no check. I said, 'That's it. I'm sending a letter to the president.'

"About a week or so later I got a call on the phone. 'This is the White House calling. Have you gotten your check yet?'

I said no. The lady said, 'We're going to take care of it now.' I was getting nowhere at our Social Security office.

"Three days after my call, Social Security called and said, 'Come right down!'

"I said, 'What's the matter; did the White House call you?'

"'Why, yes, they did! We never had a call from the White House before.'

"Well, needless to say, I got so many checks I didn't know which one to keep" (Mrs. Adelaide Milburn, Erie, Pennsylvania, July 20, 1991).

Notice why Adelaide was so effective. She went right to the top. Somehow she connected with the center of power in this country, and all of a sudden things started happening.

All of us have the same privilege, if we'll only take advantage of it. We have direct access to the throne of the universe—through the miracle of prayer.

David Cho discovered this truth as a young pastor. At the time his name was Paul Yonggi Cho, and he pastored a church of 3,000 members. Some of his members decided they wanted him to spend more time with them in committee meetings, leadership councils, and other groups. But Cho felt God was calling him to a new and deeper intimacy with Him, so he resolved to spend four to five hours a day in prayer. Some of his members didn't agree with his priorities and left. Well, the upshot of the whole thing was that a few years later his church had gone from 3,000 members to a mere 25,000 members!

Now, maybe that doesn't sound very "mere" to you, but it really was, because Cho's church in Seoul, Korea, eventually reached more than 700,000 members—the largest congregation in the world.

Would you like to know the secret behind the growth of this megachurch? When he is asked his secret, Cho says that there are three secrets to successful church growth. (Please note: you are about to get your hands on the secret recipe for church growth from the pastor of the largest congregation in the history of the planet.) Secret number 1, he says, is prayer. Secret number 2? Prayer. And number 3 is—you guessed it—prayer.

Cho notes one great difference between the church in America and the church in Korea. The church in America has much program and little prayer; the church in Korea has much prayer and little program.

David Cho is in charge of 700,000 church members, a daily Christian newspaper with a circulation of more than 1 million, 800 missionaries whom the church sends out around the world, and a large Christian university. So how does he find time to pray for several hours a day?

The answer, of course, is that it would be impossible to do all these things *without* praying for several hours a day. You see, we don't lose time in prayer; we gain time. Why? Because God can solve problems in one moment that would take months for us to solve. A very busy person cannot afford not to pray. It's like tithing. Tithing doesn't make you poorer; it makes you more prosperous. This is one of God's delightful little paradoxes, one of His surprises for those who love and obey him. Whatever we give to God He gives back better.

Martin Luther once said, "I have so much to do that I must spend the first three hours of each day in prayer." The busier we are and the heavier our responsibilities, the more important it is for us to pray.

The authors have discovered that our best and most creative ideas come to us when we spend quality time with God in prayer. If you are merely rattling off a three-minute cookie-cutter prayer in the morning, you are missing some of the best ideas of your career. Heartfelt prayer works.

Well, that's what David Cho discovered too. His prayer time became so important to him that he told his secretary never to disturb him unless his wife called and said it was an emergency. One day the president of South Korea phoned and asked to be put through to Cho immediately, but his secretary refused. When the president finally got hold of Cho the next day, he was displeased. "I want you to fire your secretary," he said.

"Sir," Cho replied, "I cannot do that. I have given her orders not to disturb me for any reason. You see, I was talking to the President of the universe, and He comes before you."

Cho's church is not the only congregation full of praying Christians in that country. All of South Korea is aflame with prayer. Perhaps one reason for this is that the nation has the sword of Damocles hanging over its head—it has for several decades faced the prospect of invasion by North Korea. Ease and plenty lead to complacency, but danger drives men and women to God. So the Christians in Korea are the fasting-and-prayer champions of the world. Wesley Duewel (*Revival Fire* [Zondervan, 1995]) states that more than 20,000 Koreans have spent 40 days in fasting and prayer. On several occasions more than 1 million have gathered to pray in Yoido Plaza—the largest prayer meetings in history.

Peter Wagner once visited another large Presbyterian church in Korea. He received an invitation to attend their early morning prayer meeting. The church had set aside a month to meet every single morning at 5:00 for an hour of prayer. The morning Wagner visited a terrible storm struck, and he suspected that not many would be present. Imagine his surprise to find 4,000 praying people filling every single seat in that auditorium at 5:00 in the morning.

As a result of all this prayer, remarkable things happen in Korea, probably the most Christian nation in the world. One chaplain transferred to Korea from Germany discovered that the same sermons that elicited little response in Germany drew crowds and changed lives in Korea. "You are coming under our prayer umbrella," David Cho explained.

The Lord can change America just as He did Korea—as soon as we are willing to pay the price on our knees.

The Assemblies of God is one of the few religious groups in the world growing as fast as or faster than the Seventh-day Adventist Church. Peter Wagner mentions a recent survey that indicates that Assemblies of God pastors spend an average of about 40 minutes a day with God, while other Protestant pastors average only 20. No wonder they're growing so fast. We don't think they should have a monopoly on the Holy Spirit, do you?

Think what could happen to your congregation if God's power was unleashed through fervent, united prayer.

~

Prayer even works in America. Sammy Tippit tells how he discovered the power of prayer in his book *The Prayer Factor* (Moody Press, 1988). The Lord brought him into contact with a man of prayer, Pastor L. L. Morris, who shepherded a small Baptist church in Monroe, Louisiana. In the late 1960s he asked Tippit to preach in evangelistic meetings in his church.

A few weeks before the meetings began he grew discouraged. Reaching the people seemed impossible. The church and community showed little interest in spiritual matters. The Vietnam War raged on. Young people were rejecting the values of their elders. Drugs and Eastern mysticism had captured their attention. Racial tensions plagued the schools. Worldly standards had crept into churches. Sammy Tippit felt defeated and helpless.

Tippit was asked to attend a prayer session with the young people. Only a few came. So he told Pastor Morris, "I believe we ought to cancel the evangelistic meetings. There's no interest. We will be wasting my time, your time, and the church's time."

But with a twinkle in his eye Pastor Morris said, "I've been praying. God has given me assurance that He is going to do something special during these meetings."

Tippit shook his head and said, "OK, but I will have to go on your faith."

When Tippit preached the first evening, there was absolutely no response. He looked at Pastor Morris as if to say "I told you so."

The pastor smiled and said, "I've been praying. It will be OK."

On Thursday night Tippit preached to about 50 people. His words seemed to have no effect on the congregation. However, at the time of invitation one of the church leaders came forward and prayed with Pastor Morris. He then went to the pulpit with tears in his eyes and asked the church to forgive him, confessing that he had failed the young people by being a poor example. The man said that God had now freed him of his alcohol problem and asked the church to pray for him.

Something wonderful happened that moment. A spirit of brokenness and prayer swept the congregation. Many came to the altar to confess sin and seek God's righteousness. On Friday evening the church was nearly full.

One of the church members had a daughter who had been arrested twice for the sale and use of marijuana and other drugs. She faced a possible 30-year prison sentence. Although she had been in drug-rehabilitation centers, she had found no cure. And she was deeply involved in the occult.

Tippit's wife, Tex, visited her and shared the gospel with her. The girl came to the services, and the truth of God's Word captivated her. After the meeting one evening she asked Jesus to come into her life and set her free from her slavery to drugs. The change in her life so impressed the authorities that they later released her into the custody of the Tippits.

By Sunday evening there was no room for the crowds. Pastor Morris said, "I've been praying, and I believe we ought to extend these meetings another week." Tippit had learned not to argue. So they moved from the church to the university campus. The first building they secured also proved too small. Again they moved to a larger building, but it was not sufficient, either.

What to do? Pastor Morris had an idea. "I've been praying," he said. "I think we ought to talk to the former Louisiana governor. He owns the local television station, and we should ask him for time on television to tell what God is doing in our city.

"I don't think he will help us," Tippit said skeptically.

But Pastor Morris said, "I've been praying, and God will prepare his heart."

The former governor gave the men two 15-minute television spots to tell what God was doing in Monroe. Then he said, "You're having problems with lack of space. Do you think the civic center would be big enough?"

"Yes, sir." Tippit was shocked.

So the former governor telephoned the mayor. "I have some young men in my office who are doing something positive in our community. They need larger facilities. I would like for you to donate the civic center to them free of charge."

The mayor agreed.

Tippit writes, "I walked out of his office that day humbled at the greatness of God. I looked over at Pastor Morris. He said nothing, but he had a smile on his face. I realized in that moment one of the great truths of the Christian life: *victory does not come from our magnificent schemes, expert publicity, or financial holdings; victory comes from the Lord.* Pastor Morris had learned that lesson years before, and it drove him to be a faithful, humble man of prayer."

During the meetings a room was set aside for prayer. Twenty-four hours a day young people could be found in that room praying. The spirit of prayer was so great that occasionally people were unable to eat.

The meetings that began with 40 to 50 people concluded with around 3,000. Both Black and White students involved in racial tension were converted to Christ, and they asked each other's forgiveness. Tippet was interviewed by the evening news several times. Newspaper articles appeared about the visitation of God's Spirit upon the youth of Monroe, Louisiana.

Out of this Tippit found himself thrust into a ministry of evangelism. It's amazing what God can do with one praying person who is not too timid to ask Him for great things.

~

Legendary golfer Arnold Palmer once played a series of exhibition matches in Saudi Arabia. His skill so impressed the king that he proposed to give Palmer a gift. "It really isn't necessary, Your Highness," the golfer said. "I'm honored to have been invited."

"I would be deeply upset," replied the king, "if you would not allow me to give you a gift." Palmer thought for a moment and said, "All right. How about a golf club?"

The next day the king had delivered to Palmer's hotel the *title* to a golf club, with clubhouse, thousands of lovely acres, and so on.

The moral of this story? In the presence of a great king, *don't ask for small gifts.*

So what have you been praying for lately? Don't misunderstand. We're not talking about asking for expensive cars and real estate. Those aren't great things—they are trivial. That would be like a kid asking his parents to give him all the candy in the store.

No, we're talking about asking for the salvation of lost souls; for an outpouring of God's Spirit on your whole family. Ask God for big things, things that glorify His name. Then stand back and watch Him work.

Our prayers make Satan tremble. Do you know of any other way to do that? Lucifer is not usually a trembling sort of guy. He doesn't appreciate being embarrassed like that, so when Satan gathers his fiends together for an infernal committee meeting, he tells them something like this:

"Do anything you have to do to keep God's people from prayer. Let them appoint committees and lay grandiose plans, but don't let them pray. Let them erect great edifices and institutions and hold large convocations, but don't let them pray. Let them publish fine magazines and produce inspiring radio programs, and let their literature evangelists sell wonderful books, but keep them off their knees. Fill their time with caring for all the things God has blessed them with. Mesmerize them in front of the television set, *but don't let them pray.*"

If prayer makes Satan tremble, then perhaps this book will inspire you to pray up such a storm in your community that you'll give Satan a nervous breakdown!

CHAPTER 3

The Uncanny Power of Praise

uthie Jacobsen hosts a weekly program on 3ABN called *When God's People Pray.* The program is taped at 3ABN studios several times a year—12 programs at a time, six a day. She brings in guests who have special stories on prayer and interviews them. But for a long time the studio lighting frustrated her. It seemed to take forever for the technicians to get it right, and sometimes she gave them grief about it— in a friendly sort of way.

In August 1996 Ruthie was attending a convention in Providence, Rhode Island, when an elderly man—let's call him Cecil—came up to her after the prayer breakfast and said, "Are you Ruthie Jacobsen?"

"Yes."

"I watch your show all the time on 3ABN."

Ruthie had never thought of it as a show.

"Well," she replied, "if you're blessed by the program, I thank God, because a lot of people pray for that program."

With a puzzled look on his face, the man continued, "But on television you're attractive. And you're charming. . . . It must be the lights!" Cecil walked away with a happy smile on his face, as if he had done a good deed.

Afterward Ruthie decided she needed to find the 3ABN

crew and tell them about her encounter. That made their day. "From now on," she said, "take all the time you need with the lights. Just get it right!"

Cecil had meant well. He thought he was saying one thing, but Ruthie was hearing another. They were not on the same wavelength (though later they became friends). We have a similar communication problem with God. We are not on His wavelength. But we have an Interpreter whose job it is to take our stumbling, stammering, misdirected prayers and translate them into the language of heaven without a faltering word. "The Spirit helps us in our weakness. We do not know what we ought to pray for, but the Spirit himself intercedes for us with groans that words cannot express. And he who searches our hearts knows the mind of the Spirit, because the Spirit intercedes for the saints in accordance with God's will" (Rom. 8:26, 27).

Without the Holy Spirit our prayer offerings to God would be something like the offerings of a devoted cat who honors her master by leaving a dead mouse on the threshold. It is the best gift she can think of, and it requires considerable effort on her part, but it is of negative value to the master.

But with the aid of the Holy Spirit our prayers and our praise are eloquent. We don't have to practice for long years before we can be allowed to actually talk to God. We don't have to "get it right" first. Our thank offerings of praise may be fumbling and faltering when they leave our lips, but when they reach His ears they are polished and fluent, bathed in the perfume of Calvary and phrased in the holy dialect of heaven.

That's a good thing, because our attempts at praise and thanksgiving probably sound just as awkward to the angels as Cecil's praise sounded to Ruthie. But to God they are a sweet aroma, just like Noah's sacrifice. Scripture says Noah built an altar to the Lord after the Flood and sacrificed burnt offerings on it. And then "the Lord smelled the pleasing aroma and said in his heart: 'Never again will I curse the ground because of man'" (Gen. 8:21).

Have you ever smelled burning flesh? Would you consider it a pleasing aroma? God did. The sacrifices of His people please Him. Today He wants much more than mere animal sacrifices—He asks us to offer our own "bodies as living sacrifices, holy and pleasing to God," as a "spiritual act of worship" (Rom. 12:1). And He seeks something else: "Let us continually offer to God a sacrifice of praise—the fruit of lips that confess his name" (Heb 13:15). Along with this comes a promise: "He who sacrifices thank offerings honors me, and he prepares the way so that I may show him the salvation of God" (Ps. 50:23). With our praise and gratitude we are paving a path to God's blessing.

So our prayers should consist first and foremost of praise. God does not like to be taken for granted. One way to do that is to forget to thank Him for His blessings. As an example of the thousands of blessings we take for granted, consider the miracle of electricity. King David, who wrote so many beautiful psalms of praise to God, did not have electricity or air-conditioning or telephones. In many ways the average American is far richer than King David. How much more gratitude do we owe God today! When is the last time you thanked God for electricity?

In 1930 electricity came to Georgia. For the first time electric lights could turn the night into day. Just after electricity arrived in his home, one happy Georgia farmer stood up in prayer meeting and offered this testimony: "The greatest thing in the world is to have the peace of God in your heart, and the second greatest thing is to have electricity in your home." What would life be like without it?

One fourth grader, when asked to write a short paper entitled "Things I Am Most Thankful For," wrote: "My glasses. They keep the boys from punching me and the girls from kissing me." When was the last time you thanked God for eyeglasses? Many people can not see clearly without them. Even today many people in the world can't get them. We who have so much should not spend most of our prayer time asking God for still more.

Don't thank God only for the pleasant things. Do you pay the doctor only when the needle doesn't sting? "All sunshine," say the Arabs, "makes Sahara." God is weaving our random trials and tragedies into a rich tapestry of His glorious grace. So when did you last thank God for, say, people you can't get along with? Scripture says in everything give thanks.

Even before we thank God for what He has done for us, we should praise Him just for who He is. God is worthy of praise whether He ever blesses us or not! From age to age, He is the most high God, ever holy, ever true, King of kings, and Lord of lords, full of everlasting loving-kindness and tender mercy. His praises never cease, and regardless of what happens to us, our whole purpose in life is to swell the chorus.

And that praise is a doorway to joy.

Sometimes—not often—the sweet spirit of praise arrives suddenly unbidden. Elizabeth Rooney is now in her 70s. Tim first became aware of her gifts through a vignette by Lucy Shaw in *Meet the Men and Women We call Heroes* (Ann Spangler and Charles Turner, eds., Servant Publications [1983]) and began to correspond with her. Much of what follows is taken with permission from her journals.

In August of 1978 Elizabeth Rooney was inducted into a lay order of Episcopal women known as the Society of the Companions of the Holy Cross. During the retreat that followed, she experienced a sudden, astonishing joy, an awareness of God's presence and His sweetness that changed her life. "I fell in love with God," she told Lucy. "It was as if my veins were bubbling with champagne." She expressed these new beginnings in her poem "Adelynrood," the name of the house of prayer at which she was inducted:

> The winter of my heart
> Melts here.
> Rivulets run
> Beneath the ice of fear.

Pierced by your warmth,
Life moves.
Spring has begun.
I feel the sun, the sun!

As this spiritual and emotional exaltation grew in the following weeks, she came to realize that the Holy Spirit had supernaturally overwhelmed her in a way she had neither expected nor asked for. One of the results was that she began to write poetry, something that she had not done since her college days. She sometimes wrote four or five poems a day, of high literary quality.

Here is an Emily Dickinson-like poem that explains her feelings about the world as she saw it with her new eyes:

I saw the world end yesterday!
A flight of angels tore
Its cover off and heaven lay
Where earth had been before.

I walked about the countryside
And saw a cricket pass.
Then, bending closer, I espied
An ecstasy of grass.

"You effervesce in me, Lord," she wrote in one poem. In her diary she wrote, "I am literally bursting with joy. I could caper like a young lamb, except that, not being a young lamb, I would look ridiculous and become embarrassed."

I didn't mean to get into this army of Yours, Lord.
I didn't bargain on joy, and on all of this love.
How do I follow these barely perceptible signals
That frequently seem to be coming to me from above?

I've been a good Christian soldier for plenty of years, Lord,
Careful and steady and dull, always marching in place.

I've made very sure that I never would get any closer,
Never so close as to hear You or look in Your face.

I thought we were only supposed to be playing a game, Lord,
There on the shore, asking "What would You have me to do?"
Now nothing about me will ever again be the same, Lord,
And it will be ages and ages before You are through!

Elizabeth had been a faithful lifelong Martha. Now God was calling her to be a Mary, and giving her a yearning for time with Him. Here's another journal entry and poem:

"This evening my heart and veins and arteries and my whole system have been filled with a joyousness I can hardly contain. I want to pray or read but feel as though I shall explode. I need to tell someone how wonderful God is!"

I haven't cleaned the cellar,
I forgot to sweep the stair,
There's a button off my jacket,
Jonny's blue jeans have a tear,
There's an old, arthritic lady
Whom I should uphold in prayer,
And I'm sitting in the moonlight,
The moonlight, the moonlight,
Adoring You by moonlight,
As if I had no care!

God has some wonderful gifts for those who make a special commitment to persevere in the practice of praise. But each person receives a different gift. Will everyone experience the kind of soul-soaring communion with God that Elizabeth Rooney had?

Yes! But not necessarily in this life. It is God Himself whom we must seek, not merely an emotional experience.

⁓

Praise lifts us up to the presence of God, and in His presence is fullness of joy (Ps 16:11). "Nothing tends more to promote health of body and of soul than does a spirit of gratitude and praise" *(The Ministry of Healing,* p. 251). So we need to praise God most when we feel like it least. We need to thank Him even when it hurts. Especially when it hurts, because praise is usually the shortest path through adversity to victory and through pain to healing.

Once upon a time, Jehosphaphat, king of Judah, woke up to the news that a huge invading army was on its way to get him. Ruined his whole day. The story is told in 2 Chronicles 20. He summoned all of Israel to fasting and prayer, and they came from every town and village to seek the Lord. Then Jehoshaphat led them in a magnificent prayer. Notice the elements of his prayer: it begins with praise, proceeds to rehearse God's saving acts of the past (in effect, saying, "Do it again, Lord"), then succinctly presents the problem:

"Then Jehoshaphat stood up in the assembly of Judah and Jerusalem at the temple of the Lord in the front of the new courtyard and said: 'O Lord, God of our fathers, are you not the God who is in heaven? You rule over all the kingdoms of the nations. Power and might are in your hand, and no one can withstand you. O our God, did you not drive out the inhabitants of this land before your people Israel and give it forever to the descendants of Abraham your friend? They have lived in it and have built in it a sanctuary for your Name, saying, "If calamity comes upon us, whether the sword of judgment, or plague or famine, we will stand in your presence before this temple that bears your Name and will cry out to you in our distress, and you will hear us and save us." But now here are men from Ammon, Moab and Mount Seir, whose territory you would not allow Israel to invade when they came from Egypt; so they turned away from them and did not destroy them. See how they are repaying us by coming to drive us out of the possession you gave us as an inheritance. O our God, will you not judge them? For we have no power to face this vast army that is attacking us. We do not know what to do, but our eyes are upon you'" (2 Chron. 20:5-12).

The very next verse says that "all the men of Judah, with

THE UNCANNY POWER OF PRAISE

their wives and children and little ones, stood there before the Lord" (verse 13). *Sometimes half of the secret of success is simply showing up!* United prayer unlocks God's power.

Evidently God was impressed, because the Spirit of the Lord spoke through a certain Jahaziel and said, in essence: "Tell you what. Don't worry about it. I'm going to take care of this Myself. You won't even have to fight them. Just get out there and show up. Don't be afraid; don't do anything; just stand there, and watch Me head them off at the Pass of Ziz" (see verses 15-17).

So that's what they did. And since the Lord was doing all the work, they had little else to do but sing and praise His name. So the king picked up on the idea and appointed some men "to sing to the Lord and to praise him for the splendor of his holiness as they went out at the head of the army, saying: 'Give thanks to the Lord, for his love endures forever'" (verse 21).

Imagine what the commander of the attacking army must have thought as he watched the approach of that peculiar army.

"Duh, what are those people doing? Are they crazy? They aren't carrying any weapons. What are they saying?"

"I don't know, sir," an orderly replies.

"Well, send someone down to find out."

"Yes, sir."

A few minutes later: "Sir?"

"Yes?"

"We know what they're saying now. Or rather, singing."

"What?"

"'Give thanks to the Lord, for His love endures forever.'"

"What does that mean?"

"Sir, they are praising their God."

"For what? We're about to slaughter them—*aren't we?*"

"They don't seem to be worried, sir. They just keep singing."

Long pause. Then sotto voce: "Uh-oh!"

Scripture says, "As they began to sing and praise, the Lord set ambushes against the men of Ammon and Moab and Mount Seir who were invading Judah, and they were defeated" (verse 22). It took three days to collect the plunder. After that they had a celebration and praise service at the Temple. The final result of this unorthodox battle plan was that "the fear of God came upon all the kingdoms of the countries when they heard how the Lord had fought against the enemies of Israel. And the kingdom of Jehoshaphat was at peace, for his God had given him rest on every side" (verses 29, 30).

What battles are you fighting right now? Have you tried the praise method of warfare? Scripture says, "Do not be anxious about anything, but in everything, by prayer and petition, with thanksgiving, present your requests to God. And the peace of God, which transcends all understanding, will guard your hearts and your minds in Christ Jesus" (Phil. 4:6, 7).

~

The book of Habakkuk is one of the choicest jewels of the Old Testament. Habakkuk lived in Judah just before the Babylonian invasion and exile. He began by challenging God to do something about the wickedness he saw all around him. "Why do you make me look at injustice? Why do you tolerate wrong? Destruction and violence are before me; there is strife, and conflict abounds. Therefore the law is paralyzed, and justice never prevails. The wicked hem in the righteous, so that justice is perverted" (Hab. 1:3, 4).

God heard Habakkuk's complaint. His startling reply, in essence, went like this: "You have a point. OK, I'll do something. I'll bring the Babylonians to punish your people for their wickedness" (see verses 5-11).

This was not exactly what Habakkuk had in mind, so he challenged God again. "Wait just one cotton-pickin' minute! How can You do that, God? How can You allow Your people to be punished by a nation that is more wicked than they are?" (see verses 12-17). And then Habakkuk resolved, like the persistent widow in Jesus' parable, that he would not let God rest until He got an answer. "I will stand at my watch and station myself on the ramparts; I will look to see what he will say to me" (Hab. 2:1).

God's answer, in essence, is "Trust Me. Their day of punishment is coming too. Someday the tables will be turned" (see verses 2-9). Habakkuk replies with a theophany in which he describes the paroxysms of nature in shocked reaction to a personal appearance by its Maker. In other words, Habakkuk is envisioning the time when God will rend the heavens like He did at Sinai and will come down and set things right. The final verses of his short book express Habakkuk's faith in God's promise: "I will wait patiently for the day of calamity to come on the nation invading us" (Hab. 3:16).

What follows is one of the greatest expressions of faith ever penned. Even as his world crumbles around him and he is bereft of the comforting evidence of God's blessing, Habakkuk makes a conscious decision to rejoice in God. "Though the fig tree does not bud and there are no grapes on the vines, though the olive crop fails and the fields produce no food, though there are no sheep in the pen and no cattle in the stalls, yet I will rejoice in the Lord, I will be joyful in God my Savior" (verses 17, 18).

A modern Habakkuk would say something like this: "Even though my husband is dying of cancer, and my son is in prison, and my teenage daughter just got pregnant, and I just lost my job; yet through all my tears tonight I will praise God for His goodness and borrow from the joy that comes in the morning."

The Thirty Years' War (1618-1648), a religious war between Catholics and Protestants, devastated most of Europe, particularly Germany. Yet out of it flowed one of the noblest hymns in the German language. The little town of Eilenburg in Saxony suffered severely. As a walled town, many refugees fled there, bringing overcrowding, famine, and disease. Plague swept through the town four times during the war. All of the pastors either died or fled except for Martin Rinkart. He alone was left to conduct the services for the dead—up to 50 in one day—until eventually the dead were buried in mass graves without services. Rinkart's wife was one of the 8,000 people who died. First the Austrians and then the Swedes sacked the town. Finally, Rinkart himself succumbed to exhaustion—but not before he had given the world a wonderful gift.

His hymn of gratitude was originally entitled "A Short Grace at Table." It is based on a text from Ecclesiasticus (also called Sirach) 50:22-24: "Now bless ye the God of all, who everywhere doeth great things, which exalteth our days from the womb and dealeth with us according to His mercy. May He grant us joyful hearts, and may peace be in our days forever." This book contains the teachings of a pious Jewish teacher named Jesus, who lived around 180 B.C., and our Lord was probably familiar with it.

Struck by the power of the text, Martin Rinkart shaped its sentiments into a powerful hymn, now translated into many languages around the world. Amid the unspeakable horrors of war, which surrounded Rinkart much of his life, he penned these glorious thoughts:

> Now thank we all our God
> With hearts and hands and voices,
> Who wondrous things hath done,
> In whom His world rejoices;
> Who from our mothers' arms
> Hath blessed us on our way
> With countless gifts of love,
> And still is ours today.

Such magnificent praise shines the more brightly because it arises out of tragedy. The powers of darkness have no reason to fear fair-weather Christians who mumble thanks now and then, but they tremble at suffering Christians who praise God anyway. It's not natural—it's supernatural.

After Job had lost everything he ever had, from out of the dark pit of his despair he said, "Naked I came from my mother's womb, and naked I will depart. The Lord gave and the Lord has taken away; *may the name of the Lord be praised"* (Job 1:21). Praise God anyway. God's glory is the important thing—everything else is small potatoes.

~

It was Easter morning, 1799, and the people of Feldkirch, Austria, were terrified. Indeed, they believed this Easter would probably be the very worst day of their lives. Outside the gates stood the army of Napoleon, and he wanted in. The citizens were ready to raise the white flag of surrender.

But the bishop of the church had another agenda. First things first, you know. In a voice trembling with emotion, he said, "This is Easter Day. This is the day of our King's resurrection. We must have one moment of triumph. Let us at least ring all the bells of Easter." Fearfully, the people agreed. Soon the sound of church bells pealing out a celebration of victory filled the air.

Napoleon's army was astounded. What could it mean? It didn't take long for the generals to conclude that only one possible explanation could account for such celebration: the Austrian army had arrived during the night to help defend the town. The bells had not yet stopped ringing when the French army broke ranks and fled.

The trembling Christians of Feldkirch were simply practicing the scriptural command to "give thanks in all circumstances, for this is God's will for you in Christ Jesus" (1 Thess. 5:18). Lest someone miss the point, Paul said the same thing again in Ephesians 5:20: "[Always give] thanks to God the Father for everything, in the name of our Lord Jesus Christ." If we do that, God will crown our lives with victory. It is not up to us to calculate the outcome, but to obey and praise God, and leave the outcome with Him.

Praise God anyway. Make this the rule of your life, and get ready for an encounter with astonishing joy.

Has misfortune so dashed your hopes and sapped your juices that you feel like crawling into a hole and dying? Just make sure that that hole reverberates with praise to God.

Sweetheart break up with you? Praise God (now you can understand His pain a little better). House burn down? Praise God (you have an eternal mansion in the heavens). Lose a job? Praise God (He's giving you a crash course in faith). Children misbehaving? Praise God (maybe someday they'll make you proud). Technicians taking too long with the lights? Praise God (you'll look better in a minute). Whether life pats you on the back or slaps you in the face, praise God. A better day is coming.

Let's say you've just won the Nobel Peace Prize—or better yet, the $1 million Templeton Award for achievement in the field of religion and faith. Praise God that because of the blood of Jesus you have an inheritance that makes such prizes look like a Cracker Jacks trinket, and ask Him to use this honor for His glory.

Or let's say you've just been thrown into prison. Praise God that He has not dealt with you as severely as your sins deserve. Praise Him that He has given you lots of free time to commune with Him, like Paul. And ask Him to use your humiliation for His glory.

You get the idea.

Far-fetched? Nonsense! Almost every year at the Voice of Prophecy Lonnie Melashenko gets a letter from some prisoner thanking God for prison, for that's where God was waiting.

In his book *Loving God,* Chuck Colson writes: "The real legacy of my life was my biggest failure—that I was an ex-convict. My greatest humiliation—being sent to prison—was the beginning of God's greatest use of my life; He chose the one experience in which I could not glory for His glory."

Colson later won the Templeton Award. Strange how God works things out.

Praise is our highest privilege. We are honing our talents for another world, tuning our hearts for the day the divine plectrum will call forth its deepest melodies. Praise is the central obsession of the angels. So if you want their companionship, do it often. Someday you'll be a candidate for the choir up there, you know. In fact, why wait? Go ahead and crash the party! Join the chorus now!

God inhabits the praises of His people. So what sort of digs does He have at your house? Maybe you are riding on top of the world, with the wind at your back. Or maybe you are in the slough of despond, with the mud in your face. Whatever.

Praise God anyway.

When you are sick and when you are well, whether you are glad or sad, rich or poor, respected or despised—build a cathedral of praise for God.

If you build it, He will come.

CHAPTER 4

Healing Prayer

In the mid-eighties cardiologist Randolph Byrd did a double-blind experiment to study the effectiveness of prayer for hospital patients. He had a computer randomly assign 393 patients to either a group that home prayer groups prayed for or to a control group that no one remembered in prayer. Neither the patients, nurses, nor doctors knew which group the patients were in. The prayer groups were told the names of their patients, and each patient had about six different people praying for him or her.

According to the report in the July 1988 *Southern Medical Journal*, the prayed for group was five times less likely to require antibiotics, and three times less likely to develop pulmonary edema, and while none of the prayed-for group required mechanical ventilator support, 12 in the other group did. The study is interesting because even Dr. William Nolan, who debunks faith healing, wrote, "It sounds like this study will stand up to scrutiny."

When Larry Dossey ran across this study, he launched into his own survey of the literature and discovered more than 130 scientific studies in the area of healing, many of which supported the effectiveness of prayer. As a result, he began to pray for his patients. Eventually he published his findings in a best-selling work entitled *Healing Words: The Power of Prayer and the Practice of Medicine* (HarperCollins, 1993).

In a subsequent work, *Prayer Is Good Medicine* (HarperCollins, 1996), Dossey quotes David B. Larson, M.D., of the National Institute for Healthcare Research in Rockville, Maryland, and former researcher at the National Institute for Mental Health. "I was told by my [medical school] professors that religion is harmful. Then I looked at the research, and religion is actually highly beneficial. If you go to church or pray regularly, it's beneficial in terms of preventing illness, mental and physical, and you cope with illness much more effectively. If you look at the research, in area after area, it's 80 percent beneficial. I was shocked."

Even more recent studies by major medical centers indicate that praying has a healing effect on the one who prays: it lowers blood pressure, eases depression, and strengthens the immune system.

Christians have known about the healing power of prayer for some time. When Lonnie Melashenko ran a series at the Voice of Prophecy on miracles, they received a number of responses describing miracles of healing. One of them concerned 30-year-old Ann Whitmore and her family, members of the Presque Isle, Maine, church.

One summer Ann, mother of three small children, found a lump in her breast. A biopsy showed the lump was malignant. Further tests revealed that the cancer had already spread to her lung, neck, and heart. Because the disease was already in an advanced stage, the doctors decided to try radiation before surgery to attempt to shrink the tumors, but Ann's condition only became worse.

In August her physician sent her to an oncology specialist in Tennessee. Ann's life became a dismal round of CT scans, radiation, bone marrow tests, and chemotherapy. By October, weak and desperately ill, she decided she had had enough. Her specialist agreed that further treatment was useless.

The last part of October her entire church devoted its service to special prayer on Ann's behalf. Along with the members and elders, she and her husband, Rodney, asked the Lord to intervene in her life and heal her. That Monday's X-rays showed no change—only the lumps, along with pinholes from heavy radiation.

The following Friday, however, was a different story. New X-rays showed no evidence of disease or radiation damage on the left side of her body at all. Convinced the machine was malfunctioning, the doctors repeated the test, with the same results. Thoroughly baffled, they decided to call in the specialist from Tennessee to X-ray her in a week. This time they found no cancer anywhere in her body, as well as no radiation damage! Upon careful examination, the six doctors discovered that even the lymph nodes they had removed to biopsy were present again, now perfectly whole!

Ann was so excited she jumped off the examination table and shouted, "He healed me!" and proceeded to explain that God had answered their fervent prayers. Her physicians decided that Ann had merely "willed herself to life" and the power of positive thinking had healed her. But it still left them puzzled as to how to finish her medical record.

~

Near the beginning of his 10-year pastorate at Paradise, California, in the early eighties, Lonnie Melashenko was asked to have an anointing service for the young daughter of one of the members. The girl, 5 or 6 years old, was almost deaf—she had some slight hearing in one ear. Numerous tests had ruled out any medical solution. The parents were beside themselves with worry and grief. The mother asked for an anointing service in harmony with the counsel given in James 5:14, 15: "Is any one of you sick? He should call the elders of the church to pray over him and anoint him with oil in the name of the Lord. And the prayer offered in faith will make the sick person well; the Lord will raise him up. If he has sinned, he will be forgiven." So Lonnie called some of his elders, and they knelt around the girl and placed their hands on her and prayed.

After the elders had prayed, Lonnie invited the little girl to pray. "I will never forget the impact of that beautiful prayer," he says. Simple, sweet, and eloquent, as if the Holy Spirit was speaking through the lips of a child, it went something like this: "Lord Jesus, You made me; You designed me; You have a plan for me. I just want to thank You for my mommy and daddy, and Pastor Lonnie, and the elders who came to pray for me today. If my life can be a witness for You, please put Your hands on my ears and heal them. Amen."

When Lonnie's turn to pray came, he was so choked up he could hardly speak. The power and presence of the Spirit were unmistakable. Finally Lonnie found his voice and asked God to take full control of her life and heal her if it was His will.

Within days the child was hearing perfectly.

In October 1997 Lonnie ran into the child's mother, who was working at Ventura Estates in Newbury Park, California, as a nurse's aide. She proudly showed him a picture of her daughter, now 21. Ever since the anointing, she said, her daughter's hearing had been perfect.

For every story like this, there are many who die in spite of the intercession of others. All three authors of this book have participated in anointings in which the anointee did not receive healing. It is not God's plan to do away with death just yet. And until He does, any physical healing is only temporary anyway.

But it is always His plan to heal the spiritually ill, as long as they are willing to meet the condition of turning away from their sin. It is in this realm that the healing power of prayer really shines.

A well-known pastor was a guest speaker one night in Atlanta to a large congregation on prayer. He talked about the importance of prayer and how, if you want something, God wants to hear from you. Prayer frees His hands to do that which He would not do otherwise. It was a powerful sermon.

An alcoholic was sitting in the back of the auditorium. As he heard about the God who never gives up on people, new hope began to creep into his heart.

After the service ended, the speaker was standing in the pastor's study behind the platform chatting with a group of elders when one of the deacons came in and said, "There's a bum out here who wants to see you."

"No, he's not a bum," the pastor replied. "He may be living that way, but he's a child of God."

"Well, he wants to talk to you. Shall I tell him you're busy? I know you have another appointment, and this fellow looks like a derelict."

"Show him in."

They brought him in. Walking up to the speaker, he said, "How old do you think I am?" The man was obviously inebriated and had trouble speaking. He appeared to be at least 55 or 60.

"I'm 36," the man continued. "Were those things that you were saying tonight true? Does prayer really get through to God, or were those just nice platitudes? I'm used to hearing from people who don't believe in what they're saying. But tonight you sounded like you really believe that God does love us and that He hears. Was that true?"

"Every word that I said was true. But it wasn't true because I said it, but because God said it. And He keeps his promises."

"Will you pray for me?"

So the elders put him in the center of their circle and knelt around him and placed their hands on his shoulders and prayed. And they asked God to come in to his life and to reveal Himself and to show him that He had a purpose for creating him.

The man staggered out.

Several years later the same minister spoke in Augusta, Georgia. A message was waiting for him at the desk when he checked into the hotel. A stranger wanted to see him at 8:30 the next morning for just a few minutes.

He went down for breakfast, then sat for a few moments in the lobby, not knowing whom to look for. Soon a well-dressed young man walked in through the door. His back was straight, he had self-confidence and assurance, and two little girls held on to his hands. They were well-dressed, happy children. As he came closer, he started singing softly, "'Amazing grace, how sweet the sound, that saved a wretch like me . . .'"

The minister stood up and shook his hand. "You don't recognize me, do you?" the young man said.

"No, I'm sorry."

"I'm the guy who staggered into the church several years ago in Atlanta. You prayed for me. And the God of heaven has answered your prayers."

Prayer heals hurting hearts. Prayer changes things.

Ruthie was invited to go with her husband, Don, to Australia and New Zealand to do camp meetings and pastors' meetings there. When they arrived, she learned of a woman whom we will call Linda, who needed her counsel.

Linda was a new Adventist Christian married to an agnostic prone to violence. The marriage was physically abusive. Linda viewed life as hopeless. As a child she had been sexually abused by a stepfather for years, leaving her scarred and broken.

Fortunately, we have a God who can heal hopeless cases, because He is Lord of the impossible.

"I'll talk to her," Ruthie said, "if you'll take a copy of this book and ask her to read it between now and our appointment on Monday."

For some reason Ruthie had slipped into her luggage two copies of a book by Henry Brandt and Kerri Skinner, *If You're Tired of Treating the Symptoms, and You're Ready for a Cure, Give Me a Call.* Her reaction upon first seeing this book had been *What an arrogant title!* But after reading it, she changed her mind. Currently it is in print under the title *The Heart of the Problem* (Boardman and Holman). The author, Henry Brandt, former owner of Ferrell ice-cream parlors, is an engineer, psychologist, and Christian businessperson.

Ruthie spoke for church service Sabbath morning. Afterward Linda asked for an appointment with her. For the rest of the weekend Ruthie remembered Linda in prayer.

The following Monday morning Linda unexpectedly brought her husband with her to the appointment. Ruthie wondered about the turn of events and was trying to decide how to handle the situation when she noticed that Linda was absolutely radiant. She looked like a different person.

"Ruthie," Linda said, "I don't really think I need to talk to you."

"OK."

"Well, I do," her husband (whom we'll call Larry) interjected. "After you gave Linda the book, she brought it home, and she spent part of the time reading it, praying, reading Scripture, and crying her way through a box of Kleenex. I could see something was happening to her. I really think I have a new wife. She said that you would understand. So I'm asking you what happened."

"Well, Larry, I think the three of us know what happened this weekend. God met her at her point of need and brought healing and hope to her heart."

"Well, I could use a little of that myself," he commented.

The three of them prayed and talked for long time. Finally Larry said to Ruthie, "I feel like we have a new sister. I've never had a sister before, but I feel like you really care about us."

"Well, Larry," Ruthie replied, "you need to know what kind of a sister you're getting. There are a couple things this sister is going to do. I'll pray for you, I'll love you, and I'll give you advice."

"It's a deal. What's your advice?"

"Well, the first thing I would do, if I were you, is read the book. Then ask the Lord in your own way what it means. Then tell the Lord you would love to know Him. The third thing is to get into Scripture."

"I can't. A long time ago I tried to read the Bible, and it was over my head. I couldn't understand it, and it didn't make sense."

"All right, start with the book of John, a few verses at a

time, and ask the Lord to show you what they mean."

"Well, I can do that."

They prayed, and Larry repeated, "I think I can do this."

Linda, excited, said, "Larry, we can do this together!" But he seemed to recoil a bit.

"No, Linda," Ruthie responded, "that's not what I mean. Let Larry do this on his own."

They hugged and exchanged addresses. Over the next few months, through the power of prayer, God turned Larry's life around just as He had Linda's.

Larry and Linda have since gone to Russia as missionaries to teach former atheists the truths of Scripture.

~

Another example of the healing power of prayer is the miraculous change God works in the hearts of those youth who get involved in prayer and ministry to others.

In the Spring of 1996 a certain young man—let's call him Mike—came from a Seventh-day Adventist academy in North America along with a group of 12 other students to help with a prayer and ministry conference at Stanborough School, and academy in the South England Conference. Five other American academies had sent a total of 90 delegates to the event.

The kids were camping in an old, unheated tent. Each group had differing expectations from the event. In England the church had billed the prayer conference as a fun-filled week of sports, and 200 English city kids, most of whom didn't know Jesus, showed up to play basketball. Some of these kids spent their time playing cards.

In contrast, the kids from a different church spent up to eight hours a day in prayer and fasting (from the media and from sugar), and focusing on Christ. These kids were not there to play (on a recent trip to Iceland they had not even taken the time to tour the island). God honored their devotion. Often several members of the group would be independently impressed with the same idea or the same texts. They prayed for a breakthrough at the Stanborough Park meetings.

Mike was not a member of the "super spiritual" group, and it soon became clear that his reasons for attending were hardly spiritual. A ringleader at his school, Mike had come to go sightseeing.

One day as the group was traveling from one place to another, a pornographic postcard dropped out of his things and landed at the foot of his youth pastor.

Before they left home, the kids had gotten together with the pastor and come up with their own rules. One of the rules was that if they changed their minds or exhibited conduct not in keeping with ministry, they would be asked to return home. The leaders decided that to maintain the spirit of the weekend they could not afford to compromise these rules in Mike's case.

A few hours later Ruthie saw the pastor talking to Mike out under one of the trees on campus for an hour. Then both of them came to her. "Ruthie, please don't send me home," Mike said. "I think I'm beginning to find God. If I go home now, I'll never find Him. I admit I came for the wrong reasons. I thought, *Here's a chance to see England.* I just wanted to see as much as I could while I was here and have fun with my friends."

Ruthie reminded him that he had been a bad influence at his school, and he acknowledged that.

"Are you man enough to tell your friends what you just told me?" she asked.

"Yes."

The youth pastor called his school group together and said, "Mike has something he wants to tell you."

"I realize that I have not come for the right reasons," the young man began, "and I haven't been a good influence. I want to change and to be a help here, and I want us all to start working together with the kids from the other schools in the group instead of working against them."

One of his friends raised his hand. "But those kids from that other school are so spiritual. They think they're so much better than we are."

"But that's not the question," said Mike. "It's what are *we* here for, and how *we* can fulfill that purpose."

Ruthie slipped out. The kids stayed for two hours, praying and confessing and imploring the Lord for help. When they left the room, all eyes were moist. The tissue box was empty, the wastebasket was full, and they were hugging her and thanking her for the privilege of being there. They were excited about what the Lord had in store for them. One girl wanted to be baptized there because her life had been changed there.

That was a turning point not only in Mike's life, but in many other lives. God blessed the conference with His power. One of the Stanborough students from the Bahamas said, "This conference was a spiritual earthquake for me."

Sometime later Mike received an invitation to go to India with the same youth pastor and a senior theology major from Pacific Union College who also had been with them in England. They were involved in special meetings for various student groups, ending with a week of spiritual emphasis at Spicer College. On Friday evening they stood in the church, speaking to the students. Mike and his older friend shared their love for Jesus and their desire to know Him better and to be more useful to Him in prayer, Bible study, and ministry.

Then Mike said, "There are three possible ways that you can respond to this week we've had together. One is to say 'I don't want to have anything to do with God.' Two, you can say 'Thanks, but I choose to go on as before; I sort of know God, and I'm going to stay in my comfortable rut.' The third option is to say 'I need a radical change, and I want God to use me.' If you have the courage to make that third decision, we will ask you to come down to the front so we can pray with you and ask God to fulfill His purpose in your life."

There was no music, no emotional appeal, just a testimony from the hearts of those two students. But 1,200 students rose from their seats and came to the front for prayer.

～

God is still healing a sick world, one person at a time. Sometimes progress seems slow. Even now we struggle in prayer for Tim's mother, Bobra (that's "Barbara" with a southern drawl), who in August 1997 was diagnosed with inoperable cancer of the liver. All three authors of this book, and hundreds of others, have been praying for her healing. Tim participated in an anointing service in September. However, as of this writing, no healing is in sight. Bobra's voice, once hearty and lilting with laughter, is now often weak and frail.

Ever since the diagnosis Carol, Tim's wife, has been praying earnestly that God would place His loving arms around Bobra and comfort her, healing her if that is His will. God has already answered that prayer in a beautiful and unexpected way.

On November 4, 1997, Bobra was lying on her side in bed. Her husband, Bruce, was lying on his back in front of her. Suddenly she felt the gentle pressure of a hand on her shoulder. She asked Bruce if he had touched her shoulder (which would have been difficult given his position). No, he hadn't. No one else was in the room.

Nothing of this nature had ever happened in the Crosby family before. The gentle touch of an invisible hand on the shoulder, though rare, is one way that angels reveal themselves to those they are sent to minister to. Many such incidents are described in the literature on angels. Such things usually happen only once in a lifetime, if that, but they are God's way of communicating His love to us during very difficult times. God seems to be saying, "Whatever happens, you are surrounded with My mercy and borne up by angel's wings."

The healing power of prayer has no limit. We can send God's healing power over any distance to those who need our help. When we pray for someone's healing and that person has surrendered to God's will, He always answers our prayer. He may not always immediately heal the body, but He restores the soul and swaddles the heart in His love, preparing it for another time, another place.

CHAPTER 5

When God Doesn't Answer

Tim and Carol Crosby were aboard a small commuter plane in Atlanta waiting to take off for Chattanooga, when Donald Trump and Marla Maples sat down in the seat directly in front of them. A chorus of whispers arose from the seats behind them, snatches of gossip and perfunctory judgment. One man asked permission to take a snapshot. In midflight Tim eventually got up the courage to ask to borrow Trump's *Business Week* magazine after he had finished reading it.

When the plane landed in Chattanooga, the airline had lost the Crosbys' luggage. Guess what? They lost Donald Trump's luggage too.

Trump recovered his luggage. Later he lost Marla.

Has God ever lost your luggage? Did He fail to deliver something to you in a timely fashion that you had asked Him for? Has He ever appeared to lack due diligence in taking care of something that you had committed to Him?

The Donald Trump story reminds us of a modern parable that goes like this: A man asked God how long a million years was to Him. God replied, "It's just like a single second of your time, My child."

So the man asked, "And what about $1 million?"

The Lord replied, "To Me it's just like a single penny."

So the man gathered his courage and asked, "Well, Lord, could I have one of your pennies?" And God said, "Certainly, My child; *just a second.*"

The problem of unanswered prayer is, to a great extent, a timing problem. We want what we want *now*, and we think if God doesn't deliver on our timetable, then He hasn't answered our prayer. But sometimes God's answer is "Just a second." Eventually we will get all that's coming to us. Keep in mind that if we got what we deserved immediately, we more likely would cease to exist. Right now we are still breathing by grace. But in God's good time we'll have it all. Someday we'll all be gazillionaires. We'll be so rich that it will make Donald Trump look like a bag lady—er, bag man (do they have those?).

If part of the problem is one of timing, another aspect is a problem of perception. We just don't know the whole story. An old rabbinic fable tells how Rabbi Jachanan went on a journey with the prophet Elijah. After a long day of walking, they happened at dusk to be passing the humble cottage of a poor man whose only treasure was a cow. The poor man ran out of his cottage, along with his wife, to welcome the strangers for the night and to offer them all the simple hospitality they were able to give in their straitened circumstances. They entertained their guests with plenty of cow's milk along with homemade bread and butter, and they were put to sleep in the best bed, while their kindly hosts lay down before the kitchen fire. But in the morning the poor man's cow was dead.

The rabbi and prophet walked all the next day, arriving that evening at the house of a wealthy merchant. They were looking forward to the comfort of his hospitality, but the merchant was cold and proud, and all that he would do for the prophet and his companion was to lodge them in a cow-shed and feed them on bread and water. In the morning, however, Elijah thanked him for what he had done and sent for a mason to repair one of his walls, which happened to be falling down, as a return for his kindness.

Rabbi Jachanan, unable to keep silent any longer, begged the holy man to explain the meaning of his dealings with human beings. "In regard to the poor man who received us so hospitably," the prophet replied, "it was decreed that his wife was to die that night, but in reward for his goodness God took the cow instead of the wife. I repaired the wall of the rich miser because a chest of gold was concealed near the place, and if the miser had repaired the wall himself he would have discovered the treasure. Say not therefore to the Lord 'What doest thou?' But say in thy heart: 'Must not the Lord of all do right?'"

We should be more skeptical of our ability to label events as either good or bad. When we say something is bad, we usually mean it is unpleasant or painful. But whether it is ultimately evil or not we cannot say, because we cannot calculate the eternal consequences.

Do you remember the Tonya Harding/Nancy Kerrigan debacle? Tonya and Nancy were both champion ice skaters. Tonya induced a friend to injure Nancy's leg, hoping to put her rival out of action.

Imagine now that you are Nancy Kerrigan. Suddenly someone you've never seen before smashes you brutally in the knee, possibly wrecking your chance for an olympic Gold Metal. As you lie there in great pain, how would you label your experience? Fortunate or unfortunate?

Now look at the event again, not through Nancy's eyes, but through your own, from your current vantage point years after the event. You have 20/20 historical hindsight. Well, which was it: fortune or misfortune? Was it a tragedy, or was it one of the best things that ever happened to Nancy? Think it over. Consider what the media attention did for her career. Remember the new circles she moved in after her healing.

And what about Tonya Harding? Was the temporary success of her devious scheme fortunate or unfortunate for her? Easy answer, huh! But wait. Sometime later, prior to the Olympics, Tonya rededicated her life to God, with tears running down her cheeks, in a church in Oregon. At a press conference shortly thereafter she mentioned that she would be skating for God—something the press was unable to understand. In an awkward attempt at reconciliation, she even hugged Nancy on the ice at the Olympics once before their competition (Nancy, obviously, was not thrilled). Let's give Tonya the benefit of the doubt and assume her repentance was real at the time.

Now let's take another look. Suppose the whole experience results in lasting lifestyle changes for Tonya Harding. Was the experience good or bad?

And what if Nancy, with her new circle of friends, decides she doesn't need God. Then what? Good or bad?

It's not so easy to compute the cause-and-effect calculus and label an event as ultimately fortunate or unfortunate, is it? We can say whether it is pleasant or unpleasant, of course, but that's about all we can determine. In fact, whether something has positive or negative consequences depends to a great extent on how we relate to it. Neither failure nor fortune is ever final. The most dazzling success carries the seeds of failure, and the most abysmal failure hides the seeds of success. The cross should tell us that. God can turn fiasco into fortune.

We could multiply examples endlessly, such as the captivity of Joseph that resulted in his exaltation and the salvation of his clan; the imprisonment of Paul that gave him time to write part of the New Testament; the concentration camp lice that kept the guards away from Corrie Ten Boom and her sister; the Bosnian shelling that resulted in the deaths of 50 people, arousing international intervention that ultimately brought a halt to the war.

The point of this is that we can never assume, just because we didn't get the answer to a prayer that we wanted, that God didn't respond to our prayer. Our story is not over till it's over, and it's not even over then, because it's never over when God takes hold of it.

~

Because we are not able to see the end from the beginning, we do not know what to pray for. "We are not wise enough to use a prayer that works 100 percent of the time," says Larry Dossey. It would be unsafe for God to entrust us with such power. Therefore, he suggests, God "scrambles the codes" by delaying His answers to some prayers and randomizing His answers to others so there is no discernible formula that we can employ to ensure a guaranteed answer.

Many authors have wrestled with the question of answered prayer. C. S. Lewis points out that prayer is not like a vending machine. Prayer is more like a child who makes requests of her parents, or a student who asks his high school principal for something. Some requests are granted; some are not. At least not yet.

Indeed, Lewis suspected that the more advanced Christians might receive less answers to prayer than neophytes, whose weak faith needed encouragement. In his essay "The Efficacy of Prayer" *(The World's Last Night and Other Essays)*, Lewis quotes an "experienced Christian" to the effect that dramatic answers to prayer tend to come more frequently at the beginning of one's Christian experience and more rarely later, then concludes: "Does God then forsake just those who serve Him best? Well, He who served Him best of all said, near His tortured death, 'Why hast thou forsaken me?' When God becomes man, that Man, of all others, is least comforted by God, at His greatest need. There is a mystery here which, even if I had the power, I might not have the courage to explore. Meanwhile, little people like you and me, if our prayers are sometimes granted beyond all hope and probability, had better not draw hasty conclusions to our own advantage. If we were stronger, we might be less tenderly treated. If we were braver, we might be sent, with far less help, to defend far more desperate posts in the great battle."

Lewis's idea that more advanced Christians are provided fewer miracles seems to be borne out in the career of the apostle Paul. While Paul was in Ephesus, a center of demonic activity, "God did extraordinary miracles through Paul, so that even handkerchiefs and aprons that had touched him were taken to the sick, and their illnesses were cured and the evil spirits left them" (Acts 19:11, 12). Much later, in his last Epistle, Paul wrote, "I left Trophimus sick in Miletus" (2 Tim. 4:20). Once he could heal crowds at a distance. Now, in the autumn of his life, it seems he couldn't even heal his own coworker. Had Paul fallen out of favor with God? Had his faith decreased? Unlikely. Paul's faith and his reputation were now established, and perhaps God needed his charismatic gifts less and his writing skills more. There is a pattern here. Ellen White's visions and incidents of healing also waned in her later life.

So, paradoxically, in some cases God's silence may indicate His respect for advanced spiritual maturity.

Three times Paul prayed for God to remove a certain pain in his life, but God refused (see 2 Cor. 12:7-10). The Scriptures are full of complaints about unanswered prayers. "Why, God, says the psalmist, are You hiding from me?" (see Ps. 13:1; 88:14; 89:46). Wake up, God! Are You asleep? (see Ps. 44:23). "Though I cry, 'I've been wronged!' I get no response; though I call for help, there is no justice" (Job 19:7). "I cry out to you, O God, but you do not answer; I stand up, but you merely look at me" (Job 30:20). "O my God, I cry out by day, but you do not answer" (Ps. 22:2). "O Lord God Almighty, how long will your anger smolder against the prayers of your people?" (Ps. 80:4). "Even when I call out or cry for help, he shuts out my prayer" (Lam. 3:8). "You have covered yourself with a cloud so that no prayer can get through" (verse 44). Even the greatest saints have had problems with unanswered prayer.

Of course, sometimes there is a simple reason for unanswered prayer. The problem may be cherished sin in the life. In his book *Why Prayers Are Unanswered,* John Lavender retells a story about Norman Vincent Peale. When Peale was a boy, he found a big black cigar, slipped into an alley, and lit up. It didn't taste good, but it made him feel very grown up . . . until he saw his father coming. Quickly he put the cigar behind his back and tried to be casual. Desperate to divert his father's attention, Norman pointed to a billboard advertising the circus. "Can I go, Dad? Please, let's go when it comes to town." His father's reply taught Norman a lesson he never forgot. "Son," he answered quietly but firmly, "never make a petition while at the same time trying to hide a smoldering disobedience."

Persistent disobedience will definitely prevent answers to prayer. Scripture often warns us about this. "If I had cherished sin in my heart, the Lord would not have listened" (Ps. 66:18). "But your iniquities have separated you from your God; your sins have hidden his face from you, so that he will not hear" (Isa. 59:2). "Then they will cry out to the Lord, but he will not answer them. At that time he will hide his face from them because of the evil they have done" (Micah 3:4).

Tim's friend Steve Mosley tells a story of his involvement in an evangelistic series in Japan that just wasn't working. No matter how hard they prayed, people were not responding. Later they discovered that two of the student missionaries were having a sexual relationship. God cannot bless disobedience.

Nor does He answer the prayers of those who are unmerciful toward others. "If a man shuts his ears to the cry of the poor, he too will cry out and not be answered" (Prov. 21:13). "When you spread out your hands in prayer, I will hide my eyes from you; even if you offer many prayers, I will not listen. Your hands are full of blood; wash and make yourselves clean. Take your evil deeds out of my sight! Stop doing wrong, learn to do right! Seek justice, encourage the oppressed. Defend the cause of the fatherless, plead the case of the widow" (Isa. 1:15-17). This applies within the marriage relationship—those who are inconsiderate and disrespectful to their spouse cannot expect God to answer their prayers (1 Peter 3:7).

Sometimes prayer is not answered "because you ask with wrong motives, that you may spend what you get on your pleasures" (James 4:3). Other times we receive no answer because we lack faith (James 1:6).

God does not expect perfection in those who pray. But He does require humble penitence for past failings and integrity of purpose for the future.

Prayer may be ineffectual because it is feeble, listless, and inconstant. Sometimes we don't get what we want because we don't really want it very badly. Charles Spurgeon compared prayer to the pulling of a rope to ring a large church bell. Some pull so feebly they hardly stir the bell. Others give only an occasional jerk. Only rhythmic and vigorous tugging of the rope rings the bell loudly enough to move the hand of God. Intensity of desire is essential. It is only the *fervent, energetic* prayer of a righteous man that avails (James 5:16). "'The kingdom of heaven suffereth violence, and the violent take it by force' (Matt. 11:12). The violence here meant is a holy earnestness, such as Jacob manifested" (Ellen White, *That I May Know Him*, p. 272). Listless Laodicean prayers do not prevail with God.

Still, many apparently faultless prayers remain unanswered. There was no lack of intensity on the part of Sandy Wyman Richert when her 7-year-old son, Trevor, was diagnosed with an incurable brain stem glioma. She begged, she sweet-talked, she cried, and she bargained with God. Lonnie interviewed Sandy for a *Voice of Prophecy* radiobroadcast that aired in February 1994. Here is her stunning testimony, given in a voice choked with tears:

"You know, what was going on in my heart was that I was trying to set up God's agenda for Him. . . . I remember talking to the Lord, and I said, 'Look, if ever the stage was set for You to be glorified, this is it! I mean, this is always a fatal condition. The glory would be given totally to You. The doctors could certainly not take credit for healing this condition that is always fatal. So many people are praying. Wouldn't it be an incredible testimony to Your power and Your love to heal this little boy?'

"I tell you, the more that we all seemed to pray, and the more people that we heard were praying, and the more fervent, and I believe, faith filled were our prayers, the quicker he deteriorated.

"The drive from my home in Santa Maria to the hospital in Santa Barbara was one and a half hours, and I drove it both ways about every three days. I would spend that drive praying out loud and crying. A couple times I had to pull off to the side of the road because my eyes didn't have windshield wipers on them.

"As I spent that time, my prayers began to change from telling God what I wanted Him to do to the prayer that said, 'Whatever You do and whatever You allow, it'll be OK with me. Because I know that I'm either going to have disappointment with You, or I'm going to have disappointment without You. I don't want to be without my son, but if I'm going to believe that You are who You say You are, and that You always operate out of love, then something very loving is going on here. And though it hurts like crazy, I have to choose whether I'm going to keep trusting You or not.'

"And when I did that, I had great peace about it. I cried about the reality of what appeared to be inevitable, but I had great peace about it.

"So often in prayer we take a card and fill it out with our agenda and give it to God to sign, when in fact what we should do is sign it and give it to God to fill out.

"The last night one of the nurses said, 'Would you like to hold him?' And they put him in my lap, and for about a half hour I just held him. It was just very difficult to watch your child fade away and get to breathing just a few times a minute. But I can tell you that the most ironic thing in that time was that I had never felt God's presence so close in my life than I did holding my son while he was dying.

"When it says that our faith cannot be shaken, I think the only faith that cannot be shaken is the faith that comes from having already been shaken. I think that God answered our prayers and is answering our prayers. It was not the answer that we felt that we wanted, and yet miracles occurred all around us, and are occurring all around us, even now, with people's hearts being moved by Trevor's experience.

It's uncanny how one 7-year-old boy could touch the hearts of so many people that he never knew.

"Someone much bigger than me is sprinkling magic dust across the country by Trevor's experience. I don't think you can explain that in any natural dimension. I think there's something very supernatural that's going on."

Sandy has recently put her story in a book, *Hold me, Help me, Heal me* (Concerned Communications, 1997).

~

God has assured us that if we ask for bread, He won't give us stones. But maybe asking for bread and getting stones is not our problem. We are far more likely to ask for stones— at the time we fancy them to be gemstones—and God, in his mercy, gives us bread instead.

Take Gus, for example. A man of the world, he was articulate, vain, and arrogant. He had a brilliant mind, and he didn't want to waste it on religion. He gave free rein to the lusts of the flesh. Gus went for all the gusto he could get, and used his finely honed mind to turn others away from God.

But Gus had not been raised that way. His mother had sung hymns to him as she nursed him. For years her tear-stained prayers for him had stormed the gates of heaven, with no evidence that God was listening.

One day Gus told his mother he was leaving town and going to the big city to pursue his career in public speaking. This is what his mother had feared more than anything else. She knew that her son would probably lose himself in the frantic pursuit of pleasure there and never return to the faith of his family. Fleeing to the church, Gus's mother fell on her knees and begged God to keep her son away from the big city. She had never prayed so hard in her life. But when the ship sailed for Rome, Gus was on it, and his mother was heartbroken.

Now, it so happened that there was a famous preacher in Rome by the name of Ambrose, and a friend of Gus's said, "You've gotta hear this guy." So he went. Ambrose was perhaps the only preacher of his day who could have reached that brilliant young mind. One day young Gus—Augustine—heard the voice of God calling him to read Scripture, and he opened to Romans 13:13,14: "Let us behave decently, as in the daytime, not in orgies and drunkenness, not in sexual immorality and debauchery, not in dissension and jealousy. Rather, clothe yourselves with the Lord Jesus Christ, and do not think about how to gratify the desires of the sinful nature." Giving his heart to God, Augustine became one of the great leaders of the Christian church.

Carl Johnson, of Kankakee, Illinois, had a son too. His country called Kenny to service in Vietnam. While his son fought fierce battles on the ground, Carl waged spiritual battles for him in another realm, praying daily for Kenny's safety. He asked that his son be brought safely home.

One day, after months of agonizing prayer, the answer came. Carl heard the audible voice of God (like Philip in Acts 8:26) say to him, "Your son is safe. I'm protecting him."

Peace took the place of Carl's fears. After that he never prayed for his son's safety again.

Two days later, as Carl drove home, he saw a number of cars parked around his home, and his dreams crumbled into dust around his feet.

His wife met him at the door.

"Kenny was killed in action," she said. "He died for a country he loved and a cause in which he believed. Just two days ago you told me he would safely return home. Now he is dead. I always believed in you. What happened?"

Carl was speechless. The voice of God had been so vivid. Unable to understand it, he asked God to help him interpret his experience.

Then he remembered when Kenny had been killed. It was about the time that God had spoken to him.

Finally Carl found peace again. God had not given him what he wanted—He had given him something far better. "Your son is safe. I'm protecting him." Carl had asked temporal security for his son. God gave him eternal security.

~

The Bible gives reasons we sometimes do not receive an answer to our prayers. Sometimes the problem is sin in our life, wrong motives, and so on. But other times God gives us more than we ask for, and we interpret it as less.

We want a million dollars; God gives us a true friend (guess which is more valuable?).

We want a human friend; God offers us intimacy with Himself.

We want an easy way out of trouble; God grants us a difficult initiation into the next higher circle of spiritual maturity.

It worked this way even with Jesus. In Gethsemane Jesus asked the Father to release Him from the unspeakable horror of the cross.

But God had something better in mind for Him: the undying love of all the redeemed. All power in heaven and earth. Endless praise. Crowns within crowns. The eternal adoration of angels. Glory beyond imagining.

But in order to give Him that, He couldn't release Him from the shame.

Kenny Johnson. Trevor Richert. From a human standpoint, God lost the luggage. Or did He? Fortunately, because God said no to Jesus, Kenny and Trevor have the brightest possible future.

"So often," says Trevor's mother, "in prayer we take a card and fill it out with our agenda and give it to God to sign, when in fact what we should do is sign it and give it to God to fill out."

When life looks darkest and the dark chasm of defeat opens up before you, just remember: things are not as they seem. Your disappointment may be God's appointment. Pain will continue to happen, and human nature will continue to shrink from it, as even Christ's human nature did. But God is good, and He will give us something better than we want for ourselves.

The sooner we can learn to pray Francois Fenelon's prayer of total submission to God's will, the better:

"Lord, I don't know what I ought to ask of You; only You know what I need. . . . I open my heart to You. Behold my needs which I don't know myself. Smite, or heal; depress me, or raise me up; I adore all of Your purposes without knowing them. I am silent; I yield myself to thee. I would have no other desire than to accomplish Your will. Teach me to pray. Pray Yourself in me. Amen."

CHAPTER 6

The Prayer God Always Answers

Prayer is a tricky thing. Even an expert can ask for the wrong thing, get it, and bring the world crashing down around his or her head. We often wish that God would grant more of our requests, but if He did, we might wish He hadn't. Once when the Israelites got tired of manna, they demanded flesh food (Num. 11). They got it—a flock of quails descended on the camp. It was the last meal some of them ever ate. Later they asked for a king (1 Sam. 8), and got that, too—at a high price. We should be careful what we ask for from the Lord. It turns out that prayer can sometimes be a sort of Pandora's box that, unwisely opened, leads to all sorts of mischief.

Fortunately, God mercifully says no to our more dangerous requests. But sometimes He lets us have what we want, perhaps to teach us a lesson. Take, for example, Hezekiah.

Although Hezekiah didn't write any book of the Bible, Scripture credits him with several other achievements—he purified Israel's worship, destroyed its idols and idol groves, and even did some fancy underground engineering to bring water into the city. Hezekiah was one of the most faithful kings of Israel. But he made some mistakes.

Hezekiah prayed two prayers. One of them saved his nation; the other nearly destroyed it. Let's take a close look at both prayers and compare them with a few other famous prayers in the Bible. Perhaps we can learn how to pray more effective prayers to the glory of God.

The story begins in 2 Kings 18. The Assyrian king Sennacherib had invaded and conquered all of Palestine. He was not exactly modest about his exploits. "What god can withstand me?" he boasted. "Tell Hezekiah," he said, "that none of the other nations have been able to stand before me. What makes you think you're any different?" (see 2 Kings 19:10-13).

When Hezekiah heard this, he went to the Temple and opened the letter before the Lord. He called all of the priests to corporate prayer. And Hezekiah himself prayed:

"O Lord, God of Israel, enthroned between the cherubim, you alone are God over all the kingdoms of the earth. You have made heaven and earth. Give ear, O Lord, and hear; open your eyes, O Lord, and see; listen to the words Sennacherib has sent to insult the living God. It is true, O Lord, that the Assyrian kings have laid waste these nations and their lands. . . . Now, O Lord our God, deliver us from his hand, so that all kingdoms on earth may know that you alone, O Lord, are God" (verses 15-19).

Notice what the issue is here: the glory of God. Hezekiah understood that Israel's salvation was not an end in itself, but a means to an end: "so that all kingdoms on earth may know that you alone . . . are God." God heard and honored his unselfish prayer. He unleashed a destroying angel upon the Assyrian army who killed possibly more men than have ever died in war in a single day, even in modern times— even from a nuclear weapon.

The story continues: "Then Isaiah son of Amoz sent a message to Hezekiah: 'This is what the Lord, the God of Israel, says: I have heard your prayer concerning Sennacherib king of Assyria. . . . Therefore this is what the Lord says concerning the king of Assyria: He will not enter this city or shoot an arrow here. He will not come before it with shield or build a siege ramp against it. By the way that he came he will return; he will not enter this city, declares the Lord. I will defend this city and save it, for my sake and for the sake of David my servant.' That night the angel of the Lord went out and put to death a hundred and eighty-five thousand men in the Assyrian camp. When the people got up the next morning—there were all the dead bodies! So Sennacherib king of Assyria broke camp and withdrew. He returned to Nineveh and stayed there" (verses 20-36).

Hezekiah's first prayer saved Israel from destruction. But his second prayer had very different results.

Shortly after the aborted invasion Hezekiah became deathly ill, and the Lord sent a message to him through the prophet Isaiah: "Put your house in order, because you are going to die; you will not recover" (2 Kings 20:1).

For some reason Hezekiah could not accept this. Under ordinary circumstances there is nothing wrong with praying to be delivered from disease. But Hezekiah had been favored with a special delivery message from God that he was going to die. He should have prayed, "Thy will be done," as Jesus did in Gethsemane. Instead, "Hezekiah turned his face to the wall and prayed to the Lord, 'Remember, O Lord, how I have walked before you faithfully and with wholehearted devotion and have done what is good in your eyes.' And Hezekiah wept bitterly" (verses 2, 3).

Previously Hezekiah had prayed to frustrate the schemes of a pagan king. But now he was praying to frustrate the plans of God. Before, he prayed for God's glory; now he prayed for personal benefit. The motive behind his first prayer was a concern for God's reputation among the nations. Now his motive was his own merit (don't be too hard on Hezekiah; he lived before the cross, and didn't know any better).

But God is gracious and tenderhearted, and what Hezekiah had said was true. Those tears touched God's heart. *He really wants to give us what we want whenever He can.* So God sent Isaiah back to tell Hezekiah that his prayer had been answered: "I have heard your prayer and seen your tears; I will heal you. On the third day from now you will go up to the temple of the Lord. I will add fifteen years to your life. And I will deliver you and this city from the hand of the king of Assyria. I will defend this city for my sake and for the sake of my servant David" (verses 5, 6).

The next verse says that Isaiah prepared a poultice of figs and applied it to the boil, and Hezekiah recovered. It is interesting that Isaiah had no qualms about using the best medicine of his day, even though God had just told him that Hezekiah would get well. The use of medical remedies in such a situation does not indicate a lack of faith, for God does not usually do for us what we can do for ourselves.

Hezekiah wasn't ready simply to accept by faith God's message through Isaiah, so he asked for a sign. When the Pharisees asked Jesus for a sign, Jesus refused to give them one (Mark 8:11-12). The Pharisees had no prior commitment to Jesus. When the devil asked Jesus for a miracle, Jesus declined (Matt. 4:3-7). But when Peter asked for a sign, Jesus gave it to him (Matt. 14:28), and likewise with Hezekiah. God answered his request for a miraculous sign, and the sun's shadow went backward.

It is a currently popular notion, heard in many pulpits, that prayer never changes the mind of God—it merely changes us. But Hezekiah's prayer clearly changed God's mind and influenced Him to do something He did not plan to do—something that apparently involved a violation of the laws of nature. God is a God of miracles, and He does extraordinary things when His people pray.

Indeed, God's answer was so miraculous that it drew international attention. Babylon sent dignitaries to enquire about the wonder. When they arrived, Hezekiah made the mistake of showing off his riches. The sad story is told in Isaiah 39. This so aroused the envy and greed of the Babylonians that they eventually invaded Judah and destroyed Jerusalem.

Many people who prosper spiritually in adversity become arrogant in prosperity, and something like this happened to Hezekiah. Second Chronicles 32:25, 26, says, "Hezekiah's heart was proud and he did not respond to the kindness shown him; therefore the Lord's wrath was on him and on Judah and Jerusalem. Then Hezekiah repented of the pride of his heart, as did the people of Jerusalem; therefore the Lord's wrath did not come upon them during the days of Hezekiah."

Even though he repented, Hezekiah's extended life had unforeseen consequences to his people. It would have been far better if he had died gracefully. Not only did he show off all the gold and silver treasure of Judah to Babylonian visitors, but he made another major mistake in his later years. He took an Arabian woman for a wife. Her name was Hephzibah (2 Kings 21:1). This woman evidently brought pagan practices into Israel.

It is significant that 2 Chronicles does not mention Hephzibah's name. The writer of Chronicles always omits any reference to mothers of kings who were foreign women. Examples include Amon, Josiah, Asa, and Manasseh, whose mothers were probably of either Arab or Phoenician origin and may have fostered idolatrous pagan religions.

Perhaps Hephzibah's name reflects her sensual beauty: "in whom is my delight." Hezekiah probably chose this woman because her beauty enticed and gratified him. He overlooked the fact that she was spiritually unfit to be the mother of a future king of Israel.

After a couple years of marriage, Hephzibah gave birth to a son by the name of Manasseh. This son would never have been born if Hezekiah had submitted to the Lord's will for his life. No doubt if Hezekiah had lived longer he would have influenced his son for good. But Hezekiah died when Manasseh was only 12.

So 12-year-old Manasseh ascended the throne of David, fatherless, confused, and troubled, and under the influence of his pagan mother. An adolescent on the throne.

Manasseh took an Arab wife named Meshullemeth from Jotbah (verse 19), no doubt with the help of his Arab mother. A flood of paganism flowed into Israel through Hephzibah. The palace garden mentioned in verse 18 for

Manasseh's burial place is named Uzza in dedication to the Arabian astral god Uzza. By marrying out of the faith, Hezekiah sowed the seeds of Israel's greatest apostasy.

Horrible sins that brought God's judgment characterized Manasseh's 55 long years of rule. Judah deteriorated spiritually and morally until it was even worse than the Canaanites whose land God had previously taken away and given to the Hebrews by promise. Verse 9 says: "Manasseh lead them astray, so that they did more evil than the nations the Lord had destroyed before the Israelites." Manasseh desecrated the Temple with pagan altars. Tradition says he had the prophet Isaiah sawed in two. At the end of his life he repented and found grace, but the overwhelming tide of evil set in motion by his life rolled onward.

Because of his wickedness, the nation lost God's blessing and ultimately its freedom. "I will wipe out Jerusalem as one wipes a dish," said God, "wiping it and turning it upside down. I will forsake the remnant of my inheritance and hand them over to their enemies" (verses 13, 14).

The glorious kingdom begun by David that had lasted for nearly 500 years was brutally terminated by King Nebuchadnezzer of Babylon. He forcibly uprooted thousands of Israelites and deported them to Babylon. He tore down the walls around Jerusalem, pillaged and destroyed the Temple, and took the remaining treasures that God had bestowed upon David and Solomon.

Hezekiah's extra 15 years of life were purchased at the cost of 2,500 years of bondage for his people. Israel was never again independent until 1948, with the exception of a century of independence under the Maccabees during the intertestamental period.

Such can be the cost of getting our own way.

～

Christians frequently ask God to save the life of someone who is dying of cancer or some other disease. We probably spend too much time praying for physical healing, particularly when the prayer is for ourselves. We want

God to postpone death a few years to fit our timetable, when we ought to be praying for the eternal life of those perishing spiritually. We care all too little about cancer of the soul. For a child of God, even a fatal disease is merely a momentary painful inconvenience, a brief interruption of a life that will outlast the stars. But the effects of sin-sickness last forever.

It is perfectly appropriate to ask God to extend life. Jesus proved that by His ministry of healing and raising the dead. But sometimes it's better to accept sickness and death at God's appointed time. When Paul asked God to remove his "thorn in the flesh," God said, "My grace is sufficient for you, for my power is made perfect in weakness" (2 Cor. 12:7-9). Was Paul any less worthy than Hezekiah? No, but perhaps God granted Hezekiah's request to show us how harmful it would be if He were to answer all of our requests for an extension of life. And perhaps God expects us to understand better, after the cross, that fellowship with Jesus in suffering is a badge of honor.

Some regard prayer as an entitlement. The privilege of prayer places an enormous responsibility upon us. We should be very careful what we do with those words from Christ Jesus our Lord: "And whatever you ask in My name, I will do it."

On the other hand, there are times when we should exercise a holy boldness to intercede for the physical life of someone needed in God's cause. James Montgomery Boice, in his book *The Sermon on the Mount*, gives an interesting example. In 1540 Luther's great friend and assistant Frederick Myconius became sick and was expected to die soon. On his bed he wrote a loving farewell note to Luther with a trembling hand.

Luther received the letter and instantly sent back a reply: "I command thee in the name of God to live because I still have need of thee in the work of reforming the church. . . . The Lord will never let me hear that thou art dead, but will permit thee to survive me. For this I am praying. This is my will, and may my will be done, because I seek only to glorify the name of God."

Shocking, isn't it! Was Luther too presumptuous in attempting to impose his will upon God? Evidently not. For although Myconius had already lost the ability to speak when Luther's letter came, in a short time he revived. He recovered completely, and he lived six more years to survive Luther himself by two months.

The same thing happened with Philip Melanchthon. Luther found his companion in a death stupor. "This time I besought the Almighty with great vigor," he wrote. "I attacked Him with His own weapons, quoting from Scripture all the promises I could remember and said that He must grant my prayer if I was henceforth to put faith in His promises!" After an hour of agonizing prayer by the bedside, he took Melanchthon by the hand, roused him, and argued him back to life. "Why don't you let me depart in peace," said Melanchthon. "No, no, Philip, we cannot possibly spare you from the field of labor yet!" After three rounds of this Melanchthon finally consented to take nourishment. Luthor had won many more years of service for his friend.

Without such holy boldness, there might have been no Protestant Reformation.

~

Luther prayed for his friends because he needed them in his ministry. But as an example of totally selfless prayer, consider a modern saint who had 22 years with little else to do but pray: Noble Alexander. He endured 22 years of Cuban prisons because someone didn't like his preaching. For several weeks he spent the Sabbath standing in a lake of sewage up to his chin because he refused to work on that day. He was once enclosed in a small box with several other men and left out in the hot sun for 90 days. During his years of prison he won many to Christ and raised up a church in every prison he stayed in. He baptized hundreds, knowing in advance that he would be punished after each baptism by being placed in solitary confinement—which sometimes meant standing on tiptoe, with spikes under his heels and water dripping on his head— for *days.*

Now, here is the point: *never once did Noble Alexander pray for release from prison.* Instead, he prayed that God's will would be done in his life and that God would use him to glorify his name.

About 1991 Tim and Carol had the privilege of having Noble Alexander as their dinner guest at Thousand Oaks, California. His happy, sparkling eyes spoke of deep joy in the Lord. Noble has a delightful sense of humor. He shared a little secret. When he and his friends were standing up to their chin in the lake of sewage, they encouraged one another with the words, "Don't make waves!"

Today Noble is a tireless worker who makes waves for the Lord.

Dan Poling, in his book *Faith Is Power,* tells of his son's departure for overseas duty in World War II as a chaplain. "Dad, I don't want you to pray for my return," the young man said. "It wouldn't be fair. I have no premonitions, but just don't pray for my return; just pray that I shall never be a coward; Dad, pray that I shall be adequate."

Chaplain Clark Poling was serving on the ship *Dorchester* along with three other chaplains: George Fox, a fellow Protestant; Alexander Goode, a rabbi; and John Washington, a Catholic priest, when a torpedo hit the ship at 1:15 in the morning on February 5, 1943. Many of the experienced GIs, contrary to orders, had been sleeping without their life jackets. The four chaplains worked to comfort the wounded, distribute the remaining life jackets, and guide men toward the lifeboats. When offered places in the lifeboats, the chaplains declined and forced their own life jackets upon unwilling soldiers who had been trained to obey the orders of their superiors. As the lifeboats pulled away from the sinking ship, the light of the final flares revealed the four men standing arm-in-arm on the deck.

Poling, writing of his son's death, said, "The only prayer he wanted was answered: he was adequate."

~

Speaking of selfless prayers, did you know that a man once actually got into an argument with God—and won! Of course, it didn't hurt his case that his argument was totally selfless. But notice the point that carried the day: What will the nations think? Study carefully Moses' masterpiece of supplication:

"The Lord said to Moses, 'How long will these people treat me with contempt? How long will they refuse to believe in me, in spite of all the miraculous signs I have performed among them? I will strike them down with a plague and destroy them, but I will make you into a nation greater and stronger than they.'

"Moses said to the Lord, 'Then the Egyptians will hear about it! By your power you brought these people up from among them. And they will tell the inhabitants of this land about it. They have already heard that you, O Lord, are with these people and that you, O Lord, have been seen face to face, that your cloud stays over them, and that you go before them in a pillar of cloud by day and a pillar of fire by night. If you put these people to death all at one time, the nations who have heard this report about you will say, "The Lord was not able to bring these people into the land he promised them on oath; so he slaughtered them in the desert"'" (Num. 14:11-16).

Moses was not finished yet. He had another trick up his sleeve (if you want to be an effective intercessor, you might consider adding these stratagems to your repertoire). Like Luther, he used God's own words against Him! He would replay God's record of compassion down through history and challenge Him to live up to His reputation.

" 'Now may the Lord's strength be displayed, just as you have declared: "The Lord is slow to anger, abounding in love and forgiving sin and rebellion. Yet he does not leave the guilty unpunished; he punishes the children for the sin of the fathers to the third and fourth generation." In accordance with your great love, forgive the sin of these people, just as you have pardoned them from the time they left Egypt until now.' The Lord replied, 'I have forgiven them, as you asked'" (verses 17-20).

Joshua, Moses' successor, used a similar ploy when Israel suffered defeat in battle at Ai. He humbled himself by tearing his clothes and falling facedown to the ground before the ark (Joshua 7:6), then he prayed, "O Lord, what can I say, now that Israel has been routed by its enemies? The Canaanites and the other people of the country will hear about this and they will surround us and wipe out our name from the earth. *What then will you do for your own great name?"* (verses 8, 9).

As you can see, this particular argument—the preservation of God's reputation—crops up in some of the greatest and most effective prayers of the Bible. Don't forget Hezekiah's first prayer: "Now, O Lord our God, deliver us . . . *so that all kingdoms on earth may know that you alone, O Lord, are God"* (2 Kings 19:19).

The prayers of Moses, Joshua, and Hezekiah show that our ultimate concern should be not for our own ease and comfort and safety and prosperity, but for God's cause in the world. That is one way of honoring God: paying Him respect. Remember, if we meet God's needs, He'll take care of ours. This principle is really just a restatement of the principle of Matthew 6:33: Put God first, and all your other needs will be supplied.

Daniel understood this too. Notice how he framed his famous prayer in Daniel 9:17-19: "Now, our God, hear the prayers and petitions of your servant. *For your sake*, O Lord, look with favor on your desolate sanctuary. Give ear, O God, and hear; open your eyes and see the desolation of the city *that bears your Name*. We do not make requests of you because we are righteous, but because of your great mercy. O Lord, listen! O Lord, forgive! O Lord, hear and act! *For your sake*, O my God, do not delay, because *your city and your people bear your Name,"* God responded to his prayer with an immediate reply. He is particularly sensitive to the prayer whose highest concern is His glory.

Near the end of His life on earth, Jesus struggled to choose between a selfish and a selfless prayer. As He spoke of the principle of self-sacrifice, it brought to mind His own destiny, and momentarily He instinctively shrank from it. "I tell you the truth, unless a kernel of wheat falls to the ground and dies, it remains only a single seed. But if it dies, it produces many seeds. . . . Now my heart is troubled, and what shall I say? 'Father, save me from this hour'?" (John 12:24-26).

As Jesus thought about His death, suddenly the spectre of the cross loomed before Him and He mysteriously began to experience the power of darkness. He felt the shame and tasted the bitter cup. A terrible dread came over him, and He shrank from that hour.

Jesus broke off His discourse and sat in deep, brooding silence. His disciples saw a change come over Him and felt the gloom. Their Master did not usually hide His feelings. "He could not witness a wrong act without pain which it was impossible to disguise *(The Desire of Ages,* p. 88)." Sometimes He wept in public. Now he shivered at the horror of the cross. "What can I say, Father? Shall I ask You to deliver Me from this hour?" He wavered like a reed shaken by the wind. He argued with Himself, "How can I pray this prayer? This is why I came into the world; I came here to die."

Finally the struggle was over and the victory was won. Christ prayed: "No, it was for this very reason I came to this hour. Father, glorify your name! Whatever it costs, use My shame for Your honor." God honored that prayer with an immediate answer, in the form of a voice from heaven: "I have glorified it, and will glorify it again" (John 12:28).

It's not easy to pray that prayer. Can we sacrifice everything we have ever lived for, even our good name if necessary, for God's glory? Can we say "Father, nothing counts except Your honor"? Someday perhaps the test will come. We may be raised to the pinnacle of success to glorify God. Or we may die a shameful death for the same purpose. What difference does it make as long as the Lord's name is glorified?

God's glory. It's not the main thing—it's the only thing. "Glorify Your name" is the prayer God always answers. Christ has adopted us as His children, so He has vested His reputation in us. The universe is watching to see what we will let Him do with us.

Both Jesus and Hezekiah faced death. Neither of them wanted to die. Neither felt they deserved to die. Both prayed for release from death. But one prayer came down on the side of self-preservation, the other on the side of self-surrender. One prayer resulted in the destruction of Jerusalem and the disgrace of Jehovah; the other resulted in the salvation of the world and the glory of God.

Which prayer is yours today?

CHAPTER 7

The
Wow Factor

Give us this day our daily bread." Why did Jesus include such a petition in His model prayer? He could have made scores of seemingly less mundane and more essential requests—such as "Fill us with Your Spirit." After all, why do we need to pray for something that depends so much on our own effort? And why should we have to constantly remind God that His creatures need daily food?

Could it be that we need to remind ourselves every day that He is the source of all things—even those things that seem to depend on our own effort?

Sometimes under extraordinary conditions all of our human efforts fail, and it is necessary for God to work a miracle to supply us with our daily bread. In Bible times God performed several great miracles to supply food to hungry people. Through Moses God sent His people manna, and through Jesus He multiplied the loaves and fishes for a crowd of thousands. The Lord has repeated both of these miracles on a smaller scale for believers in this century. First, the manna. The story is retold in Mabel Tupper's book *Angels at Pincher Creek*.

It happened in Angola in 1939. Fifteen years earlier Pastor and Mrs. W. H. Anderson had established the

Adventist mission in an area where no missionaries had ever been. The mission grew rapidly, with God's blessing, and by 1939 the Central Angola Mission involved about 400 people. But that year there was a severe famine. No rain fell for months, and the food supply ran out.

The director of the mission, Carlos Sequeseque, was traveling at the time, but his wife called the people together to pray. She read to them the story of the manna and said that, if necessary, God could once again send manna. There followed a session of intense prayer.

When they arose from their knees, her little girl ran outside and saw several European men standing there. "Little girl," they said, "your prayers have been heard, and God has sent you manna. See, it is all over the ground. Pick up some. It is good."

The girl picked up some of the substance to eat and went back inside. After she told her story, the entire group rushed outside. The Europeans had vanished, but the ground was covered with a white substance that tasted just as the Bible describes it in Exodus 16:31. It was found only on the 40 cleared acres of the mission property. The manna reappeared for three successive mornings, though no one ever saw where it came from. However, it did not spoil like biblical manna. The people filled many containers, and it lasted until the rains came and a new crop of maize was harvested. Pastor Cardy brought a container of it to America seven years later, and it was just as fresh as ever.

Skeptics who heard this story said the "manna" had been exuded from a certain type of gum tree, but no such trees existed on the mission property, only orange trees.

The miracle of the multiplication of the bread was repeated in 1988 in the Takoma Park, Maryland, Seventh-day Adventist Church. Mrs. J. L. Holbert tells the story in the *Columbia Union Visitor*, December 14, 1988.

It was Communion Sabbath. The deaconesses had prepared 18 trays of Communion bread—or so they thought. But when the trays of bread were counted that morning, there were only 16. No one knew what had happened to two of the trays.

One tray was always held back in case of an emergency. So the deacons took 15 trays of bread, moving from aisle to aisle, offering bread to the worshipers from the trays they held in their hands.

Coon suggested that he and Danny Miller, another deacon, stand at either end of the row and pass the trays as they do with the offering basket. They watched. They prayed. The worshipers served themselves.

Some bread remained on the tray at the end of the second row, so they started down the third.

We'll never make it, thought Harry House, the presiding elder who watched the parishioners take the bread, one by one. But after the third row, the tray still had bread left.

The deacons started down the fourth row. Norman's heart beat faster as he eagerly watched and prayed. He was tense, then excited. The bread was lasting!

He and Danny could hardly believe what they were seeing. After all five rows had been served, almost as much bread remained on the tray as in the beginning.

"It was incredible," Harry House said afterward, "to actually witness the multiplication of 'the five loaves.'"

Both of these stories involve emergencies. But Gina Wahlen's answer to a "daily bread" prayer, while it involved a need, fell short of a genuine emergency. Here it is in her own words:

"The day started early, with the sun peeking over the rocky tops of the Grand Tetons. It didn't take long for my husband and me to realize it was going to be a beautiful (and very warm) day.

"Taking the boat across Jenny Lake, we decided to go for a short morning hike, before the weather was too hot. We wound our way around massive rocks, through grassy meadows, toward the peaks, where the scenery became increasingly beautiful and the path increasingly long.

"The sun was now overhead, and my stomach was reminding me that lunchtime was near. However, planning on just a short morning hike, we had foolishly left food and water behind. Since we were well over halfway to the top, we decided to proceed despite our lack of supplies.

"During the next hour I started talking with God. 'Lord, my mouth is so dry. In fact, it hasn't been this dry since I had my tonsils out—when they gave me a shot that turned my tongue into cotton. I realize it's because of our own carelessness that we don't have anything to eat or drink, but please help me. I'm so thirsty and hungry.

" 'I know that You know my needs, and I would certainly be happy with just some bread and water, but Lord, I don't mean to be presumptuous, but what I'd really like is crackers, cheese, and juice. I know it's a crazy thing to ask way out here, but I just thought I'd ask anyway, because I know that nothing is too hard for You.'

"Feeling quite foolish for asking God for such a favor, I walked on in silence. Before long it was clear I could not hike any farther. Asking my husband to go on, I wearily sat down on a rock, relieved for a place to wait in the shade of several trees.

"Before long another adventurous couple came by my rest area. Grateful for the shade, they stopped briefly and told me about their hiking expedition. I could see from their gear they were prepared hikers—with food, water, and other supplies.

"As they were leaving, the man said, 'We have some food with us. It's just some crackers, cheese, and orange juice. Would you like it?'

"Hardly believing what I was hearing, I eagerly accepted their kind offer.

"That was the most delicious meal I have ever eaten, because I knew it was a direct gift from a kind heavenly Father who even cares about seemingly silly requests."

If it's not food, it's water. It happened during Operation Desert Storm. Marine Major General Charles Krulak found his men without an ample supply of water after General Norman Schwarzkopf's unexpected change in strategy required them to move to new terrain. Repeated attempts to dig for water failed, even after consulting local experts. Krulak exhausted all resources but one: the regular 7:15 a.m. prayer session to which he invited any staff who wished to come.

One day a well suddenly appeared overnight beside a road built by the Marine Corps. A colonel discovered a pipe rising out of the ground, with a cross formed by a protruding crossbar. At the base of the pipe was a brightly painted red pump, a green diesel generator, four new batteries still wrapped in plastic, and 1,000 gallons of diesel fuel—a type of fuel not used by the American forces—stored in a tank above the ground.

The equipment was ready to run, and when Krulak pushed the start button, the new German-made generator turned over and the water started to flow, providing almost exactly the 100,000 gallons of water a day needed.

Krulak and 20,000 of his men had repeatedly traveled that road and could not have missed the highly visible well. Was the well put in place overnight by the Saudis? Regardless of how it got there, it was a providential answer to prayer.

~

Most of God's workaday answers to prayer involve supplying necessities to people who are at the end of their rope and cannot help themselves. But sometimes God breaks all the rules and does something really fancy, even extravagant. Just like we send flowers to those we love, sometimes God sends a bouquet of blessing to His children, with all the frills.

Emily—who asked that her real name not be used—sat in a small plane on the runway waiting for takeoff. Her heart sank as she heard the pilot announce that the flight would be extremely bumpy because of rough weather. "I wish I could promise you a smooth trip," the pilot said, "but I can't because there are thunderstorms in the area."

The takeoff was fairly smooth. Once in the air the flight attendant began to prepare to serve the drinks. She had just started passing out the peanuts when the pilot's voice came over the intercom and asked her to sit down, explaining that they would be passing through heavy weather for the duration of the flight.

Emily doesn't like to fly, particularly in small planes. In her anxiety she recalled Roger Morneau's testimony of a recent miracle in his life involving travel. In his book *Beware of Angels*, Roger, who is an intercessory prayer warrior in frail health, tells of how he and his wife were driving through heavy rain in the mountains of Oregon. The spray raised by passing trucks obscured their vision. Roger began silently quoting Scripture and praying for relief from the heavy downpour that made driving difficult and dangerous. Suddenly it stopped raining over the northbound lane of the interstate only. For the next two hours and 10 minutes they drove along in a small dry envelope, with rain falling on each side of them.

Hmmm, Emily thought, *if God could do that, then perhaps He could create a smooth path in the sky for her plane. You could do that, God . . .* It was more a thought than a prayer.

After 15 minutes of smooth flight, the pilot once again spoke over the intercom. "Folks, I apologize because you haven't had your beverage service, but they are reporting a lot of turbulence on both sides of us. It's going to get worse as we near our destination."

Meanwhile the plane flew on through a placid corridor of air.

Sometime later the pilot's voice again came over the intercom. "Well, folks, I want to apologize again for the lack of service. Planes on both sides of us were reporting heavy turbulence, but somehow," he said, using the exact words of her prayer, "we seem to have found a smooth path through the sky." The plane landed without incident.

The retreat to which Emily was traveling turned out to be a deeply spiritual weekend. The multiracial crowd of more than 300 demonstrated a tremendous sense of unity, and there were many small miracles. It was a turning point for Emily, who had been deeply worried about a particular problem in her life. She felt her anxieties melt away into peace. God had her in His hands.

~

Larry Stephens' family had a weather-related problem too. When Larry attended Southern Missionary College (now Southern Adventist University), his studies left little time for family recreation except on Sabbath. One Sabbath afternoon he took his wife and two small children over to the student park. They were enjoying the shady grass between the old rock quarry and a stream when a sudden, fast-moving, violent thunderstorm took them by surprise. A large tree provided some shelter until the rain became too heavy, then Larry and his wife spied an overhanging cliff, picked up the children, and ran for refuge. Protected from the storm, they soon became aware of the rapidly dropping temperature. Their daughter Debbie, 4, looked up and asked, "Daddy, let's ask Jesus to stop the rain; I'm cold."

"Sure, honey," said Larry. As they knelt on the ground, with the rain coming down in sheets, Larry knew, even before the first word of Debbie's prayer, that she was in for a disappointment. As she prayed, he cast about for some way to explain why God had not answered her prayer. *That's it!* he thought. *Jesus had to decide whether to stop the rain for us or let it keep raining so the farmers could grow more food for those starving children in China!*

When Debbie said amen and opened her eyes, she could hardly see the trees a few feet outside their shelter. Larry, ready with his story, was startled by the new look of doubt in her eyes. He couldn't allow mistrust of Jesus to develop in his child's mind.

"Why didn't Jesus stop the rain, Daddy?"

Her father's plan changed in the twinkling of an eye. He reminded his daughter of the story of Joshua leading the Israelites across the Jordan River, which they had talked about in family worship that week. Larry had emphasized that the waters of the river did not part until the priests with the ark of the covenant stepped into the water. They had to demonstrate faith by their action. "Debbie," he concluded, "we didn't show we believed Jesus would stop the rain, did we?"

"How can we do that, Daddy?" She was puzzled.

"Let's pray again, and this time when we are finished, we'll go home."

As Debbie prayed, her mother and father silently joined in, anxious that God would honor her childlike faith. As they opened their eyes, the storm continued unabated. Joining hands, they walked toward the entrance.

"As we left the shelter," Larry wrote, "a few drops of rain may have fallen on us; I don't recall any. Directly before us was brilliant sunlight. The storm continued to the right and left. Looking up, we saw a large horseshoe-shaped depression in the cloud above."

The seed of faith that Debbie gained from that experience grew and bore fruit a few years later, when Larry was teaching in Tallahassee, Florida. That month the budget was tight, and just before morning worship Larry asked the family to be especially careful until payday. Debbie spent the rest of the day with a friend, and that afternoon Larry went on an errand across town. He was driving down a lonely road a few miles from home when a small piece of green paper blew across the road. Stopping the car, he walked back and found a $10 bill. With a thankful heart, he continued on his way.

That evening after Debbie returned from her friend's house, Larry said, "Debbie, guess what I found today?"

Without batting an eye, Debbie replied, "Daddy, you found $10."

How could she know? thought Larry. A rapid mental review of the day's activities provided no answer.

"Young lady," he asked, "how did you know I found that money?"

With the nonchalance of a child to whom this was no big deal, she replied, "At worship this morning I asked Jesus to help you find $10."

Today Pastor Stephens teaches at Forest Lake Academy in Apopka, Florida.

~

Does God sew up torn clothes? Well, maybe sometimes. Texan Betsy Rubsamen believes in miracles. They are, she says, impossible things that happen anyway. Here is her story:

"I'd like to tell you about a miracle that happened while I was preparing my daughter, Ann, for college. I hope that you can accept it as an illustration of God's concern for us even in what appears to be the smallest details of our lives.

"Ann and I were shopping for school clothes late one afternoon and happened upon a dress that we felt would be just perfect. Upon close examination, however, we discovered a scissors-like cut near the left side seam. We decided to buy it anyway, believing that I could repair it reasonably well enough to pass inspection. After I got home I examined it again and figured that I would take material out of the hem to patch the cut. I then laid it aside, thinking that I could tackle that little project the next morning.

"Then next morning I could not find the cut. Feeling awfully foolish and somewhat blind, I walked into Ann's room to ask her to help me find it. It shouldn't have been that difficult to find on a solid beige dress! To our amazement, Ann couldn't find the cut either. She looked up at me and asked, 'Mama, did you pray about this dress last night?' I replied something to the effect that my only prayer was that the Lord would help me to do all the little things I needed to do to get Ann ready to go off to school. In total disbelief, Ann and I looked at one another. Could it be? We dared to think, *O Lord, who would believe?* It really didn't matter; we believed! There was no other explanation for the now-perfect condition of that little dress.

"I've never been able to relate much to God's parting of the Red Sea to ensure His people's safety from the hands of Pharaoh. But after that small and uplifting event, I realized that God cares about me and all my needs, no matter how insignificant.

"We nicknamed that dress the 'holy dress.' To this day it reminds us of God's love."

And speaking of clothing . . .

When Ruthie was living in Oregon, a pastor's wife came up to her one day at camp meeting and told her how much it had embarrassed her to attend the pastor's banquet the night before in an old dress. "I haven't had a new dress in three years," she said. Still, she felt God was blessing her.

So Ruthie started praying for money to buy clothes for more than 100 pastors and their wives in the Oregon Conference. Her husband, Don, was the president of the conference, but she didn't tell him about her prayer, knowing he loved to solve problems by himself. Impressed with Mueller's success in supporting his orphanages by secret prayer without ever soliciting donations, she decided to try it herself.

Shortly after, a physician approached her. "Ruthie, could you use some money for clothing for pastors and their wives? I have $10,000 for that purpose, provided that no one ever knows where it came from."

"Yes!" she exclaimed. "I want you to know that you are the direct answer to prayer. Nobody but God knew about this."

She did some figuring and realized that that wasn't enough, so she kept praying. Monday morning when the check arrived at her office, it was actually for $15,000.

It was just before Christmas. So she wrote a letter to pastors offering them either a gift certificate or reimbursement for clothing receipts. A few pastors called and said they didn't need the money. Others came in after Christmas and thanked her. She passed a note on to the donor: "This is from the Lord."

The Lord prompted the physician to repeat his offer four years in a row at Christmas. Then Ruthie stopped praying about it. December days trickled by, and no money came in. On December 23 she suddenly realized the need, fell on her knees, and asked God to forgive for forgetting to pray about that request. That afternoon the physician called. "You know, we haven't done anything this year, but I want to do the same thing again." Ruthie sent letters out that day.

The Lord is not able to do as much as He would like to when we don't pray specific prayers. We are on enemy territory, and perserverance in prayer tells God and the enemy that we are serious about our requests.

That same physician once walked into Ruthie's office when she was praying for money so pastors could attend a conference. "Ruthie, do you need money?" he asked.

"I've been praying and asking the Lord for it!"

"Well, I've just left a check for $10,000 for you."

"Let me tell you what it's for."

"Oh," said the physician, turning to go, "I don't care what it's for."

"If God will answer my prayers," Ruthie says, "He'll answer anybody's. And I believe He answers in tangible ways to give us faith to ask for the big things, such as courage to witness, eternal life for others, and assurance of salvation for ourselves."

~

Maisie Albright Key, of Santa Rosa, California, writes that one of the lower front teeth of her 6-year-old son had come in perpendicular to the others. "I earnestly prayed that it would be straightened," she wrote, "for if his mouth was ever hit, his lip would be cut. We had no money for an orthodontist. I left the matter in the Lord's hands and went to bed. It may seem strange, after such earnest desire on my part, but I thought no more about it for the next two days. Then when I remembered I looked at my son's teeth, and they were perfectly in line. Thank the Lord!"

We hesitate to share some of these stories because God does not usually work in such ways. But we have discovered that we cannot put God in a box. God does whatever He wishes. Sometimes in His infinite wisdom He says no to big, significant requests, and sometimes He says yes to small, whimsical ones.

The Chudleighs were vacationing in southern Oregon with no planned itinerary. They drove their station wagon from one campground to another, and eventually turned back south down Highway 1, where they camped among the redwoods just off the northern California coast.

Early on a Friday afternoon, having lost track of time, they pulled into a campground and asked if there were any open campsites. The attendant gave them a funny look and said, "No campsites are available unless you have a reservation. This is the Fourth of July weekend, and you would have had to make reservations at least three months ago to get in. You're not going to find anything this late."

The reply came as a bit of a jolt, as they were 1,000 miles from home with no plans for the evening. They drove down the road to two other state parks. Same story. They tried several motel units. No luck.

As they headed toward the last and largest campground, Becky Chudleigh said, "I'm going to pray about it." She did. "I think the Lord's going to give us a camping spot," she declared.

Her husband said nothing, but his skeptical propensities went into high gear. *What exactly is the Lord going to do here? Is He going to create a new space? Will the camp directors look at their map and say "Oh, wait, we've got a new space here we've never noticed before"? Or is God maybe going to vaporize one of the campers? This is silly.*

At last they reached a very large campground on the west side of Highway 1. As they approached they could see a line of cars exiting the campground full of sleeping bags and tents and kids in the back seat with glum looks on their faces. Nevertheless, Becky said, "I prayed, and I'm sure the Lord's going to give us a camping spot," so they joined the line of a dozen or so cars at the entrance to the park. As they inched forward, they watched as each car ahead of them would pull up to the booth, roll down their window, and talk to the attendant, who would shake her head and then hand them a piece of paper. Then the car would do a U-turn and pass by on the way out, glum faces and all.

Finally the Chudleighs arrived at the booth. Gerry rolled down the window and said, "Just wondering if you had an empty campsite." The attendant started to reply when suddenly someone tapped on her window. "Excuse me a minute," she said. In a moment she was back. "Well, you're in luck. These people just phoned their friends who were coming to stay in the campsite next to them, and they're not coming. So we have an opening for you."

They paid the fee and drove through the gate, watching in their rearview mirror as a long line of cars continued to do U-turns. The Chudleighs had a delightful weekend. And Gerry, realizing that God was a little bigger than he thought, has become a lapsed skeptic.

～

The Toppenbergs also liked to travel. They owned a 22-foot cream-and-green Terry Trailer that had provided many happy hours for them. It had become an essential part of the family, and Donna could not bring herself to part with it.

Her husband, Glenn, had other ideas. At the time they lived in Stoneham, Massachusetts, and he was a physician on the staff of the New England Memorial Hospital. He had grown weary of the major repair bills on their 1972 Ford LTD that resulted from pulling the trailer. Even though the car had a heavy-duty towing package, so far they had replaced one transmission and three rear ends. Finally, at Norridgewock, Maine, the camshaft broke, damaging the cylinders, and they had to have the engine rebuilt at considerable expense. At that point they agreed that they could no longer afford to pull the trailer with the LTD. They would either have to get a new car (Donna's suggestion) or sell the trailer (Glenn's suggestion).

Unfortunately, they could not agree. Glenn felt that they could not afford a new car, and it would be too risky to attempt to pull the trailer with a used car of unknown capabilities. Donna could not bring herself to part with their trailer. Glenn agreed not to sell the trailer without his wife's permission. They prayed over the issue, but mutual agreement seemed unreachable.

Seeing that he was fighting a losing battle, Glenn began

to consider what sort of car they might need in case they decided to buy one and settled on a GMC Suburban. He obtained a book listing the wholesale dealer cost of the car with the various options he would need.

One morning, after many weeks of indecision, Glenn decided the time had come to do something. So the Toppenbergs knelt together and prayed for God's guidance. Glenn prayed that God would somehow put a stop to the transaction if it was not His will for them to have a new car.

Armed with the wholesale price list, Glenn was on his way out the back door in the basement to the local GMC dealer when the front doorbell rang. At the door was Pastor Doug Cross, whom Glenn and a group of other doctors in the area had hired as a physician's chaplain to follow up their interests. Glenn and Doug were good friends, and Glenn had briefly mentioned the problems he had had with his Ford, but had never expressed to Doug any intention to buy a new car.

Inviting Doug in, Glenn asked what he could do for him. "Well," he said, "I have a brother with me who is visiting from Texas, and he has a GMC Suburban that he would like to sell so that he can afford to go back to school. I was wondering if you might be interested or know of someone who was."

"You may find this hard to believe, but I was just walking out the back door to go buy a Suburban! This book under my arm is the dealer price list! We just prayed that the Lord would guide us to the car He had for me if this was His will," Glenn said. And then he added cautiously "And if He is answering our prayers this directly, I wonder if it might not even be the right color—a light green?"

"Well, it's a cream color with green trim," Doug replied.

They went out to look at the car, and discovered that it was painted the exact same cream color with the exact same green trim as their trailer!

The asking price was just what Glenn had earlier decided was the most he could really afford to pay—considerably less than the price of a new one would have been.

Their trailer, pulled by their miracle car, gave them many more years of pleasure.

~

Finally two lost-and-found prayer stories. The first one is from Mrs. Edith Roper, of College Place, Washington. When her son Don was between 12 and 13 years of age, they lived in Portland, Oregon. Her husband pastored the Tabernacle Seventh-day Adventist Church there, but that day he had gone to a ministerial meeting in College Place, Washington. Don and Edith decided to drive along the Columbia River to an area above Multnomah Falls and hike around there for a while. Where they parked, the sand was quite deep. They locked the car and began a long hike. But when they returned, the key was missing.

After frantically searching their pockets and the area, they returned again to the car. Realizing there was nothing they could do, as it was already too late to hike down for help, they bowed their heads and asked the Lord to help them, believing He would answer their prayers. Immediately they felt a strong impression to dig in the sand under their feet, where they found the keys buried almost four inches deep.

Ray Woolsey is a retired editorial vice president of the Review and Herald. His answer to prayer happened on Christmas weekend around 1952. At the time he was a single pastor in southern Alabama, and his fiancée, Challis, was a nursing student at Washington Sanitarium in Takoma Park. It had been six months since they had been together. That Christmas Ray's parents, who lived in Collegedale, Tennessee, invited Ray and Challis to join them over Christmas weekend.

The Woolseys' property extended from Ringgold Road up to the top of White Oak Ridge. On a cold Sabbath afternoon Ray and Challis decided to climb the ridge. A neighbor's dog chose to tag along. They started climbing through the woods up the steep hill, with no path to follow. About three fourths of the way up, they sat down to rest, leaning back into the soft oak leaves on the steep slope. They were huffing and puffing from the climb, and Ray's glasses started to steam over. Taking them off, he laid them on the leaves beside him. Meanwhile, the dog cavorted around them. After 20 minutes or so Ray reached for his glasses, but they weren't there. A long and careful search finally led them to conclude that the dog must have taken them.

Ray realized that he had to go back to his church district the next day, and ordering glasses in those days was a complicated affair that could take weeks. Finally, having exhausted the possibilities in the immediate vicinity, the pair stood up and prayed earnestly that God would show them where the glasses were. Placing himself under God's direction, Ray decided he would move laterally 10 steps along the side of the mountain. He then made a quarter of a turn facing down the mountain, bent over, reached down, and touched the glasses under the leaves.

"That one experience has served as an anchor point in my life," Ray says. "I know that, come what may, the Lord is there and is prepared to take care of me."

We need to balance such stories with some good advice: we should not count on God in advance to rescue us from our own stupidity. Usually He doesn't. Furthermore, cars and camping spots are not the sort of thing that is the main focus of the daily prayers of mature Christians. Nevertheless, one thing we can be sure of: God is sympathetic to our problems. Whether the problem involves our daily bread, our daily transportation, or just a set of keys, God will provide. He owns the cattle on a thousand hills, and the hills under the cattle, and the stars over the hills. And prayer is the key to His riches.

Just one more thing. If God will work such amazing miracles in regard to things that mean little to Him except as tokens of His love for us, then *think how much more He will do when we ask for things that mean everything to Him—namely, the salvation of lost souls!*

CHAPTER 8

Opening Hearts Through Prayer

A ndrews University had 14 feet of snow during the winter of 1977. Ruthie Jacobsen was teaching in the School of Nursing, and her husband, Don, was a professor at the SDA Theological Seminary. That winter Don and Ruthie received an invitation to go to Jamaica, and they jumped at the chance to get out of the slush. They found substitutes to cover their classes for a week and took off for a tropical adventure that would be more exciting than they planned.

In Jamaica Ruthie encountered a large assortment of delicious tropical fruits. Ruthie loves fruit. She grew up on a fruit farm in eastern Oregon. All week long she felt a strong desire, almost a compulsion, to take fruit back for her boys, Randy and Jerry. But when she shared the thought with Don, he reminded her that it was illegal to take fruit on the plane.

Soon it was time to go, so Don put Ruthie on the plane to Miami (he had to stay for some meetings). As she flew over Cuba with fruit on her mind, it occurred to her that a lot of tropical fruit must be shipped to Miami, so maybe she could find some there.

After deboarding in Miami, she went into the customs office, which was packed with people. The line didn't seem to be moving, but before long Ruthie arrived at the desk. The agent asked her several routine questions about her luggage without inspecting it. The interview was unusually fast, and she soon found herself walking out of customs and into the terminal. Stepping up to a kiosk, she asked, "Can you tell me where I can find a fresh fruit market?"

"I'm sorry, but I'm not here to answer that sort of question," the attendant replied. "I can't help you."

Just then a rather diminutive man wearing an airport badge walked up. "I happened to overhear your question," he said. "I can tell you where you'll find a wonderful, fresh tropical fruit market. You can't take a bus—you'll have to take a cab." He proceeded to draw her a small map.

She took the map and thanked him. Hailing a cab, she gave the map to the driver, eagerly anticipating the smell of fresh tropical fruit.

"Lady," he said, "I know Miami like the back of my hand, but I can tell you there is no fresh fruit market at this address."

"Well, I don't know Miami at all," she replied, "but this man seemed so sure that I think we ought to go there. But if we don't find anything, you'd better bring me right back. By the way, how much is this going to cost?"

"About $8 if we hurry."

Earlier Ruthie had discovered that she had only one $20 bill in her wallet.

When they arrived at the spot, there was no fruit market. So the driver took her to a supermarket. It had no tropical fruit either, and all the while the meter was ticking. Anxious about the cost, Ruthie said, "Let's go back to the airport." Then she added, "But first let's go back to the address on the map and if you find a small road or driveway, let's take it."

Soon the driver turned onto a small road. A few hundred yards down the road was a huge fruit market.

Ruthie was worried about her dwindling finances, so she quickly chose a few pieces of fruit, mentally tabulating the cost. Meanwhile she noticed that the cab driver was putting fruit in bags too. "I have chosen some wonderful fruit for you," he said, "because I am from here, and I know what's good." So she took a few things out of her bag and convinced him they had enough.

Ruthie suspected she didn't have enough cash to cover the cost. When she asked the cashier "Would you possibly take a check?" he leaned back and roared with laughter. In a condescending voice he said, "Do you know where you are? This is Florida. We don't take checks here. Where are you from?"

"Michigan."

"Well, this is Florida, and we don't take checks. But . . . I'll take your check."

As the cabdriver stood by open-mouthed, Ruthie wrote the check, picked up her fruit, and returned to the cab. Before the driver even got his door closed, he turned around and said, "Lady, you were lucky."

"No, that wasn't luck. I prayed."

"Well, I pray too, but my life is falling apart."

She prayed as she talked. "When we come to the valleys in our lives—and we all have them, and sometimes they seem so deep—God is there and He's saying, 'I still love you; I care, and I have a plan for your life, and you can trust Me.'"

"You know," the cabdriver replied, "my mother was a praying woman. She was a Seventh-day Adventist. So were my father and my brother, and I used to be. I was in the military, and on three occasions I nearly lost my life. And I promised the Lord if He would just keep me alive and keep me safe, that I would live a Christian life, and that He could be in control. But . . . I really don't know what happened. It was subtle. I got married, and we were so happy, and I guess the temptation was 'Who needs God?' Things were going so well. I guess I thought I could make it on my own, but slowly my life started to unravel, and I couldn't stop it.

"Now I'm divorced, and I seldom get to see my two daughters. I have three jobs to try to make ends meet, and nothing is working for me. My life is falling apart. But just last night I knelt down by my bed and said, 'Lord, I once had a relationship with You, and someone must be still praying for me.' I told the Lord about this one sin in my life that I didn't think I could ever give up. I surrendered it last night, and I gave everything to God."

The cabdriver looked at Ruthie in his rearview mirror, with huge tears rolling down his cheeks, and asked, "Why am I crying?"

"Well, this is a pretty big moment for both of us. God has arranged for you and me to meet today."

"Just last night I prayed that prayer, and here you are today, telling me God loves me."

"Sir, there's one more thing I need to tell you."

"What's that?"

"I'm a Seventh-day Adventist."

"No!"

"Yes!"

While steering with one hand, he reached into the back seat with the other and shook hands with his new sister in Christ.

All the way back to the airport they talked about God and how faithful He is and how He has a plan B if we mess up.

Just before she left, Ruthie asked, "Can I pray with you?"

"I'd love it," he said.

Together they thanked God for being such a big God. And then, of course, they argued about cab fare.

"One thing I will not do," the man said, "is accept any money from you this morning."

"But the Lord has provided this cab fare, and He wants you to have it," Ruthie retorted.

Finally he took it. Then he picked up the bags of fruit, asked for a box, and packed the fruit carefully. They shook hands and said goodbye.

A few moments later, as she was standing in line to check her luggage, Ruthie felt a tap on her shoulder. "I have to tell you one more thing," said the cabdriver. "This is the happiest day of my life."

Ruthie's obsession for fruit was God-given. But it was really an obsession for another kind of fruit.

A life of prayer is a life of adventure! When people commit themselves to God in prayer, there is no telling where He will lead.

～

Ruthie has been sponsoring teen prayer conferences around the United States, with amazing results. The teenagers lead out in them. Prayer makes them bold.

About 400 teenagers and several hundred adults attended one of these teen prayer conferences. A young man about 16 years old stood up in the pulpit and said, "Before I give my sermon, I have a word for you from the Lord." At this some people in the audience squirmed in discomfort, including Ruthie.

"You adults have all the education and the experience, the understanding of the community, and you know what works and what doesn't. We young people have energy, and the faith, and we're willing. As I see it, there's a big work to do, and you can't do it without us, and we can't do it without you. So let's get together. Now, that was from the Lord. The rest of this is from me."

Here was a young man so sure of his relationship with the Lord that he knew the difference between what was from him and what was from God, and was unafraid to speak about it in public. And these young people, by relying on personal prayer, have begun to establish a track record of ministry that more experienced adults might envy.

In April of 1995 a prayer and ministry conference convened in Paradise, California. A local group of academy students had recently gone on a mission trip to Guatemala. As a result of that trip, the kids had voluntarily begun to observe certain spiritual disciplines involving daily prayer and Bible study. The kids drew up the guidelines themselves: a minimum of 30 minutes a day in individual prayer and Bible study, an hour or two each week meeting together in corporate prayer and study, and some sort of outreach ministry to others. If you want to belong, they told each other, you work out of your overflow, not out of your lack.

The young people found that God began to work in a

powerful way in their lives. The church started to see baptisms. They were so excited that they decided to go to the pastoral staff and share with them their plans for studying the Bible. The pastors could see that they had a genuine love for Jesus, so they asked, "Why don't you take our dwindling Wednesday night prayer meeting and teach the adults how to study Scripture the way you do?"

So they did. The teenagers began to lead out in the prayer meeting, and attendance began to grow.

One night two women dropped in to prayer meeting. Looking around, they saw that everyone was already clustered into small groups, and they started to leave. One teenager by the name of Tommy followed them and asked, "Where you going?"

"We're late, so we'll just wait until next week."

"Oh, no! The three of us will be a group."

As they were discussing the passage of Scripture for the evening, Tommy noticed that one of the women—let's call her Sharon—was crying. "What's wrong?" he asked.

"I have a friend tonight over in the hospital who is dying of cancer. And I just wish she could have been here tonight to discover the beauty of what I have learned about Jesus."

"Is she a Christian?"

"No."

"Then you need to go and share this with her."

"I can't. That is a total impossibility. I have never in all my life led anyone to Jesus. But I've heard that you kids are doing this all the time, and that you have baptisms as a result. Will you come and do it for me?"

"No. You have to do it, and I'll tell you why." Tommy took her through the five steps of ministry as Jesus practiced it, based on *The Ministry of Healing* (p. 143):

1. Jesus mingled among the people as one who sought their good.

2. He got acquainted with people and found out what their interests were.

3. He filled a need (such as the shortage of wine at Cana).

4. He won the confidence of the people.

5. Then He said, "Follow Me."

Tommy continued: "That's why I can't do what you want me to do. I haven't earned the right. But you are her friend. She loves and trusts you."

"Tommy," Sharon cried, "I can't do this."

"Get in my car," the young man said. "I'll drive you to the hospital, and I'll teach you everything you need to know on the way." On the way he explained how to make a gospel presentation and told her what scriptures to use.

"Tommy, I can't do this."

"Look, you know everything that I know . . . OK, look, I'm going to find a chair and put it outside the door of this room, and I'll be praying that God will give you the right words to reach the heart of your friend."

When Sharon walked in and greeted her friend, they both burst into tears, because they realized that death would soon separate them. So Sharon started telling her friend about the passage of Scripture they had just studied and that it had blessed her heart and that she wished her friend could have been there with her.

"But I've never had anything to do with God," her friend protested. "Why would He want me now?"

"Well, why did God want the thief on the cross? It is God's nature to bless."

They kept talking. Eventually Sharon asked, "Would you like me to pray with you and ask God to take control of your life?"

"Yes."

Sharon prayed the sinner's prayer, and her friend repeated it after her. Then they wept again.

Walking out of the hospital room, Sharon found Tommy bent over, praying in his chair. "Tommy, this works!" she exclaimed.

The next day the woman died. But she was safe in the arms of Jesus. What might have been merely a sad conversation in a patient's room had turned into a transaction sealed in heaven. And Sharon would never exchange that experience for anything in the world.

~

Prayer empowers people. The only thing we have to fear, as Franklin Roosevelt put it, is fear itself. Prayer emboldens God's children to witness, breaks down barriers, turns stumbling blocks into stepping-stones, and opens closed hearts, making them receptive to the approach of the One to whom they belong.

Just the suggestion of prayer can be a powerful bridge to the heart. An effective ministry opener is to ask an acquaintance, "How can I pray for you this week?" Few people will take offense at someone wanting to pray for them. And often they will open up their hearts and take you into their confidence.

At a Sunday morning prayer breakfast during a recent conference at Cohutta Springs, Georgia, the moderator asked for testimonies. A pastor from Alabama—let's call him Fred—stood.

"Last year when I was here," he said, "you encouraged us to find a prayer partner, somebody with whom we had a lot in common. So I found another pastor from Illinois whom I had never known before. The two of us became partners and good friends."

Fred went on to report that they had followed the suggested plan of praying for each other daily and praying together once a week. But one week Fred was having a terrible time in the ministry. Some of his members were criticizing him, and he was discouraged.

That Sabbath morning he woke up and thought; *I'll call my head elder this morning and tell him I'm just not well. I'll ask him to take the service today.* He rationalized that he needed the rest.

Just then his phone rang. It was his prayer partner in Illinois. Fred dumped the whole load of his pain on his friend, who understood the situation because he was up to date on the circumstances. The other pastor started praying with and for Fred, thanking God for all the ways He had used Fred ever since he started in the ministry, for all the lives he had touched. He praised God for the way His purpose was still unfolding, and thanked Him for what He was going to do that day through Fred's ministry.

By the time they hung up, Fred was eager to jump into the shower and get to church and see what the Lord was going to do through him that day!

Scripture says, "Where two or three come together in my name, there am I with them" (Matt. 18:20) and "Though one may be overpowered, two can defend themselves. A cord of three strands is not quickly broken" (Eccl. 4:12). Deuteronomy 32:30 says that while one man can chase a thousand, two can put ten thousand to flight. Partnering is an important way of multiplying prayer power.

Even strangers are often open to the suggestion of prayer. How much we miss by not interacting with people we don't know. All around us are individuals without hope, yet more open to salvation than we think. A little push from us would bring them into the kingdom. There are a thousand simple ways we can reach out and share our blessings with others. If the Holy Spirit is leading, our interaction with others will have eternal consequences.

Years ago a rash young high school student, a shirttail relative of Lonnie's, was standing on the high school playground with his cronies, telling off-color stories. The kids were playing "Can You Top This One?" and it was Dick's turn. Just as he was about to unload his X-rated joke, he noticed a 9-year-old kid standing nearby, listening to the older boy's stories. This bothered him because he had no desire to contribute to the delinquency of a minor, but he went ahead with the story anyway. Then somewhat miffed, he turned to the kid and demanded, "And what do you want?"

The kid asked, "May I pray for you?"

Dick found himself at a loss for words. All he could think of was "Sure, go ahead, kid. Pray."

Dick never forgot the opening words of the young man's

prayer. "Hi, God!" Dick was aghast. He had never heard anyone address God like that before. He wondered if the earth might open up and swallow them all, or that lightning might strike them all dead.

But the young boy continued to pray. He said some nice things, without any thees or thous. And when he finished, he said, "See Ya later, God!"

Then as five teenage mouths stood agape, the young man turned and began to walk away, then stopped, turned back, and said, "I think you'll like God. He's a great guy!"

The participants at these prayer conferences do more than just pray. At the longer conferences they spend a whole day in ministry, or half a day at the shorter conferences. People are asked to participate at their comfort level. Some of the kids visit hospitals; some visit nursing homes. Some go on a prayer walk in large communities. When they walk by a tavern, they pray for the people inside. When they pass a high school, they pray for the students and teachers.

At a recent teen conference held in Kettering, Ohio, a group of teens went with one adult to witness at a mall. The idea was to get acquainted with the shoppers and pray with them if the occasion presented itself, "mingling with people as one who sought their good."

One extremely shy teenager was very uncomfortable with such an approach. He wandered around, praying silently as some of his friends walked up to tables in a food court and sat down and talked to the diners. They seemed so at ease. *I could never do that!* he thought. So he stayed to himself and asked God, "Lord, is there anybody here for me? I don't know what I'm doing." Glancing upstairs to the upper level, he saw a bench with someone sitting on one end. So he decided to sit down and think and pray.

The young woman beside him seemed pleasant and friendly, so he started talking to her. After the small talk, he asked, "May I ask you a personal question?"

"Sure."

"Do you believe in prayer?"

"Do I believe in prayer! Let me tell you something that happened in my life that changed my attitude toward prayer forever. Ten years ago I had a baby at Kettering Medical Center who was dying. The doctors had given up hope.

"One afternoon a group of Seventh-day Adventist young people came into my hospital room and said they were there singing and visiting patients. So we got acquainted, and I told them about the heartbreaking situation I was facing. And they said, 'Could we pray for your baby?'

"These kids stood around the bed and lifted my little one up to God's throne. They asked God to touch that little life and bring healing if it was His will. Everyone else had given up. But this group of young people asked God for the impossible. As a result of the prayers of those teenagers, my child was healed. And today I have a healthy 10-year-old because those Adventist young people prayed."

"I'm a Seventh-day Adventist," the young man said. And then he took the opportunity to pray with her on that bench and thank God for what He had done 10 years ago, and to ask God to continue blessing the woman's family.

That night when everyone returned to share their stories, his friends were amazed to see this shy young man, who had never been up front, eagerly jump up and tell what had happened to him that day. He could not keep the story to himself. It just bubbled out of him and became a great source of praise that evening.

Such testimony services are Spirit-filled events. A recent one held in Keene, Texas, began at 7:30 p.m. and lasted until midnight. One young participant put it this way: "You cannot imagine how much power there was in that room. There were tons of kids who thought it was cool to be excited about God."

We are seeing the beginnings of an exciting, prayer-and-ministry-centered revival going on right now among the youth in the Seventh-day Adventist Church in North America. The wind of God's Spirit is starting to blow.

CHAPTER 9

Cover Your Loved Ones With Prayer

In response to extraordinary prayer, God does extraordinary things. One of the most remarkable intercessory prayer success stories of all time comes from James Dobson. His great-grandfather spent an hour a day in prayer for his descendants. For decades he walked the hills behind his house, pleading with God for his children and his children's children. Then one day a most unusual thing happened: God interrupted his prayer and told him that he had prayed enough about the matter. His prayers had been answered, and *all of his descendants down to the fourth generation would belong to Him.*

James Dobson is a fourth-generation descendant. So far, he claims, not only have all of his relatives been Christians, but all of the males of the clan have been ministers. When James decided to go into psychology instead of the ministry, some of his relatives thought he was abandoning the faith!

Just think what the prayers of that one obscure Christian four generations ago have done to turn the hearts of the fathers to the children and the children to the fathers across the nation! Persevering prayer is a powerful thing: it can sway the destinies of generations to come.

John Newton was for many years a wicked man and a

slave trader. But, like young Augustine, he was a prisoner of grace, hemmed in by the prayers of a devout mother. She died of tuberculosis when he was only 7, leaving him to a godless father and stepmother. But 22 years later her prayers found their mark. Newton wrote the autobiographical song "Amazing Grace" and was responsible for the conversion of William Wilberforce, who almost single-handedly persuaded Parliament to abolish slavery.

Think about it: slavery was abolished in part because Newton's mother prayed.

~

The most frequent prayer request that Lonnie receives at the Voice of Prophecy concerns wandering loved ones. This has been a serious problem throughout Christian history. We frequently hear disconcerting statistics about the percentage of youth who leave the church. (It is often left unsaid that some of these prodigals later return, though figures are hard to come by.)

There is a remedy.

You may not have accumulated the prayer time that Dobson's great-grandfather did for his children, but it's never too late to get started. In fact, it's never too early, either. If you don't have children yet, start praying now for your future children. Start a bank account of prayer in heaven for them.

Here are several promises you can claim for your children. The first one is Isaiah 44:3: "For I will pour water on the thirsty land, and streams on the dry ground; I will pour out my Spirit on your offspring, and my blessing on your descendants."

If you have children, don't let the Lord rest in peace until He grants to you this promise. Challenge Him to make it good. In Scotland a few years after the turn of the century, several deacons in a country church stormed the gates of heaven with the promise of Isaiah 44:3 for hours on end, determined not to cease until they had their answer. Suddenly at around 3:00 in the morning the entire building shook like a leaf and the lights came on in every home in the valley as

all the coal miners suddenly awoke under intense conviction of sin. A great revival spread throughout the region because of the prayer of those deacons.

In Galatians 3:7-9, 29 we read that those who believe in
Jesus can claim the promises of God given in the Old
Testament to the nation of Israel. Here's another one: "But
this is what the Lord says: 'Yes, captives will be taken from
warriors, and plunder retrieved from the fierce; I will contend with those who contend with you, and your children I
will save'" (Isa. 49:25).

Isaiah 54:13 declares: "All your sons will be taught by the
Lord, and great will be your children's peace." Generations
of intercessors have used such promises as blank checks
given by the Lord to draw on His inexhaustible love account
in heaven. By claiming them you can facilitate the gift of the
most wonderful thing in the universe—eternal life—to the
most wonderful people in the world: your own loved ones.

When we pray for the salvation of others, we can be sure
we are following God's will. It's good to say "not my will,
but thine be done" when requesting a personal favor or
physical healing, but this is not necessary when we ask for
the salvation of others. It is almost a lack of faith to say "if
it is Your will" when interceding for souls because God has
already said that He wants everyone to be saved (1 Tim. 2:4).
So we can pray for the salvation of others with absolute confidence that we are in His will, and we can thank God for the
answer in advance.

Does this mean that God will force someone to be saved?
Does He take away their free will? No. It is possible for a sin-
ner to resist the most persistant prayer. On rare occasions
God even tells an intercessor to stop praying for someone
who has determined to go their own way, as He ordered
Jeremiah to stop praying for Israel (Jer. 7:16; 11:14; 14:11).

Charles Finney, in his book *Answers to Prayer*, relates that
he had been interceding for a prominent man in the community who had come under a sense of conviction. One day
he was tearfully pleading with God for his friend only to

find the door of heaven slammed shut in his face. God seemed to be saying, "No, I will not hear. Speak no more of this matter." The next morning Finney saw his friend, a legislator, and brought up the question of submission to God. The man replied that it was out of the question for the time being, as he was politically committed to cast a vote that was incompatible with Christianity. Then Finney understood. The Holy Spirit had gone from the man, and he never again came under conviction.

But until God tells you to stop praying, don't ever give up on your loved one. That person may in the end resist the Spirit of God, but the Divine Hunter is going to unleash His most powerful artillery to bring that soul into His kingdom.

In fact, Charles Finney himself was converted because someone didn't give up on an unpromising case. Finney learned that "some members of the church had proposed, in a church meeting, to make me a particular subject of prayer, and that Mr. Gale had discouraged them, saying that he did not believe I would ever be converted, that from conversing with me he had found that I was very much informed upon the subject of Christianity, and very much hardened." Fortunately, the church prayed for Finney anyway.

~

Hudson Taylor was a headstrong young man who had a praying mother. She was away from home for several weeks, staying with some friends. One Saturday afternoon she felt a special burden for her only son. Leaving her friends, she went alone to pray for his salvation. She spent several hours on her knees, until her heart was suddenly flooded with the joyful assurance that God had answered her prayers.

Meanwhile, back at home Hudson, out of boredom, had randomly chosen a book from his father's library to read. As he read he was arrested by the words "The finished work of Christ." He began to wonder why the author had used those words instead of others, such as the atoning work of Christ. Then the memory of familiar truth long neglected touched his heart. He was converted by the thought that Christ had provided a full and perfect atonement for sin, and all he had to do was to accept His finished work. The thought brought him to his knees and impelled him to a life of sacrificial service to his King.

He wanted to be the first to share his newfound joy with his mother when she returned two weeks later, but he was too late. "I know, my boy, I know," she said as she hugged him. "I have been rejoicing for two weeks in this glad news." The Holy Spirit had already told her.

Then Hudson discovered that his sister had made a vow that she would give herself to prayer every day until her brother was converted. She made this commitment just one month before his conversion (Howard Taylor, *Hudson Taylor's Spiritual Secret* [Moody, 1989]).

Hudson Taylor became known as the father of modern missions. He spent his life working for China and made prayer the basis of his ministry. Indeed, later in his career, when the ministry he had established needed more workers, he sent a cable to all the workers and to London that said "Praying for hundred new workers in 1887."

Four years earlier they had prayed for 70 new workers over a three-year period, and God had supplied them, but 100 in one year was unprecedented. Hudson also prayed for $50,000 of extra income without solicitation, and that the donations might come in large sums to keep down correspondence because of his small office staff.

So what actually happened in 1887? Six hundred men and women applied to serve as missionaries, of which 102 were chosen to serve; $55,000 extra income came in without any sort of appeal, and it came from just 11 sources.

God doesn't play favorites. If you are engaged in mission for God and are putting yourself to the stretch and find yourself in need, He'll do the same for you that He did for Hudson Taylor. Of course, God does not always give us the answer we want. Did Hudson Taylor ever pray for something he didn't get? Was everything always smooth sailing for him? Not at all. In 1900 nearly 200 Protestant missionaries and their children were martyred in the Boxer Rebellion, along with thousands of Chinese Christians. During this fierce uprising many of Taylor's converts were massacred and his mission stations were burned—all in spite of Taylor's prayers.

One thing this suggests is that God chooses to save lives rather than buildings and that His primary objective is saving souls. In other words, it is always God's will to reclaim the soul of your loved one for His eternal kingdom, and He will move heaven and earth to do so. But it is not always His will to keep them alive here on earth. We learn that from the book of Job, too.

Job, a righteous man, interceded for his children on a regular basis. Job 1:5 says: "When a period of feasting had run its course, Job would send and have them purified. Early in the morning he would sacrifice a burnt offering for each of them, thinking, 'Perhaps my children have sinned and cursed God in their hearts.' This was Job's regular custom."

Every day he covered them with the blood of the Lamb, which is what every believer should do every morning for every member of their family by invoking the blood of Jesus upon them. But that didn't keep Job's children from dying, for in a single day every one of them was killed (verse 19). But they were covered with the blood.

Job struggled with the injustice of it all, railed at God, and pled in vain for release from his troubles. But the heavens had turned to brass.

God did not answer until Job once again found himself interceding for others—this time his tactless friends. "And the Lord turned the captivity of Job, when he prayed for his friends: also the Lord gave Job twice as much as he had before" (Job 42:10, KJV). Remember, *if we meet God's needs, He will meet ours.*

~

Intercessory prayer does not necessarily make life easier. Sometimes its full effects do not show up until the next generation. Take Sue, for example. She used to spend an hour each morning and another hour each evening in private prayer for her children, of which there were more than a dozen in the home most of the time. The family was poor, and Sue had her share of unhappiness and misfortune. She had constant differences of opinion with her husband, Sam, a minister, one of which resulted in his leaving her for a time. A poor manager of money, he was once jailed for indebtedness. Not long after he got out, their house burned down. Her daughter Hetty got pregnant out of wedlock, then quickly married a drunken plumber as a cover for the pregnancy. The rest of Sue's daughters also married unhappily.

Life wasn't easy for Susanna Wesley.

But her prayers were not in vain, because two of her sons, Charles and John, founded a great movement that called men and women to holy living and changed the spiritual climate of England and the world. The Seventh-day Adventist Church is descended, to a great extent, from this Wesleyan tradition.

Perhaps you have a wandering daughter like Hetty Wesley. Here is a story to restore your courage. Jeannie, Ruthie's friend, lives in Oklahoma. Jeannie and her husband had done their best to live consistent Christian lives and to raise their children in the Lord, but somewhere, somehow, something went awry.

"I think I have some understanding of how Hezekiah must have felt," she told Ruthie, "for he tried to be a godly leader, but he had a son named Manasseh. Our daughter Ginger went all the way through Christian schools, but when she moved to Dallas, she lived the life of Manasseh."

Every day Jeannie went to the Lord in prayer. She took to Him her special promise that she believes God gave her in Job 5:24: "You will know that your tent is secure, for you will visit your abode and fear no loss" (NASB).

"Years ago I claimed this special promise, and You have blessed my family," she told the Lord. "But now Ginger is living like Manasseh, and I have suffered loss and my tent is not secure." Yet every time she prayed she got up from her knees with peace that God was sharing her burden and had heard her cry.

One day her teenage son Christopher said, "I need to borrow some money."

What she thought was *If our children would just pay back the money they'd already borrowed, we would be very wealthy people!* But what she said was "Why do you want to borrow this money?"

"There's a new Christian cassette out that has a song on it about returning to the God who still loves you and returning to the people who love and care for you, and I want to buy it and send it to Ginger." Keep in mind that Ginger never called home. Whenever anyone made contact, it was always Mom, Dad, or Chris who made the call.

So she gave him the money. He sent the song to Ginger.

A few weeks later the phone rang. Jeannie answered, and it was Ginger. They talked, then the daughter said, "Mom, I've been thinking that maybe I would like to come home and get a job there."

Jeannie's heart did flip-flops, and her mind went into overdrive. Darting a prayer to heaven for divine help, she decided she should be nonchalant, not eager and pushy. "Honey, we'd be happy to have you at home with us."

Ginger said she would work it out with her current job and let us know when she would be home.

"I thought I had done a pretty good job of appearing nonchalant," she said later, "but I danced around the house saying 'Yes! Yes!' because I knew God was working."

Ginger came home. The family experienced some strained moments, but Jeannie and her husband tried to be accepting and supportive of her. One day out of the blue Ginger said, "Mother, when do you have devotions? I know that prayer and Bible study are an important part of your life, but I never see you. When do you do it?"

"Well," her mother replied, "the reason you don't see this is because it's very private and personal, and I usually have my quiet time very early in the morning, before anyone else gets up."

"Well, some time I just thought we could do it together, but I'm never up at that hour of the day."

Jeannie was thrilled to discover that Ginger wanted to have that experience with her. "Honey, whenever you feel it would be a good time, I'd be happy to arrange to have worship together. When would be a good time for you?"

"Well, I'd probably like to do it about 11:30 or 12:00 at night."

Jeannie groaned inwardly, but said, "Ginger, if that's a good time for you, that's perfect." So they set a date for the following night.

At that point Jeannie found herself becoming nervous and uptight. "Don't let me do the wrong thing and get pushy and blow it," she prayed.

When they got together, Jeannie said, "Here's a nice chapter. Do you want to read it, or should I?"

"You can read it, Mom."

When they finished reading, Jeannie said, "Now let's pray. Do you want me to pray, or . . ."

"You pray."

Jeannie prayed. Afterward Ginger kissed her mom good night and went to bed. Disappointed and discouraged, Jeannie sat still. "Lord, there was no meeting of hearts here. It was just an empty, rote experience. I'm afraid Ginger was bored."

Jeannie didn't hear the Lord saying anything, but she had an inkling that God might be saying, "You know, I was a little bored Myself."

As she was thinking what a dismal failure she had been, the Lord seemed to impress her with "Why don't you show her how you have devotions, just as I showed Moses how to build the tabernacle according to the pattern."

"I couldn't do that, Lord! That is my holy of holies."

God was silent.

"All right, if You'll give me another chance, I will show her how I have devotions."

Jeannie kept praying. One day Ginger came in and asked again if they could have devotions together.

"Sure, honey, but we're not going to do what we did last time."

"We're not?"

Jeannie led her daughter over to two chairs in the corner of the bedroom. They sat and opened the Bible, and she began singing the Steve Green song based on Philippians 1:6, "He who began a good work in you will be faithful to complete it."

"Oh, Mother, I love that song. Teach me that song."

So they sang it again and again. Before long the Lord seemed to nudge her and say, "OK, she's got the song. You can show her now what you do for devotions."

So Jeannie began using the words of the Psalms to praise the Lord, personalizing them for what the Lord had done that day. Next she started confessing. She acknowledged thoughts and words and actions that were wrong, and thanked God for forgiving the sins of her youth. Then she brought her petitions before the Lord, praying for her children and others. She went through her usual routine.

"Mom, I think I could do that," Ginger said. Then the girl read a passage from the Psalms.

They hugged and each went off to bed. This time Jeannie had an entirely different feeling about the whole prayer experience. She thanked God for giving her the courage to let go of her self-consciousness and share the personal experience she had with Jesus.

A short while later Jeannie was in the kitchen when Ginger came up to her and said, "Mom, I'm ready to commit my life to the Lord in radical obedience the way you have." And Jeannie had the privilege of leading her daughter in a prayer of commitment to Christ.

Ginger started attending church and dating Tom, a Christian. One day her mother heard the girl singing, "'He *could* begin a good work in you.'" Later Ginger said, "Tom didn't know that you could have devotions that way."

If you have read this far in this book, then God has no doubt already begun a good work in you and in the lives of those loved ones for whom you are praying. And if you keep praying, He will faithfully complete it. Your devotional life may not take exactly the same form as Jeannie's, but whatever spiritual disciplines you use—journaling, singing, praying out loud, etc.—God will bless your efforts to seek His face. But day in and day out, consistency is important. The destiny of another individual may be hanging in the balance.

~

We have immediate access to a vast reservoir of untapped prayer power. Claim those promises. Spend the time in prayer. If you can't do it on your knees, then pray while you're walking. But "pray without ceasing" (1 Thess. 5:17). Keep in mind that this does not mean "Pray without pausing," but "Never stop praying." God is calling us to relentless prayer. I like the way Winston Churchill put it, in perhaps the shortest speech ever given. The meeting was running overtime that day, so the great orator decided to greatly abbreviate his speech. It is essential counsel for intercessors. "Never give in," he said. "Never, never, never, never."

Ron Mehl, in his book *Surprise Endings* (Multnomah, 1993), tells the story of a remarkable answer to an intercessory prayer. Roger Simms had just left the military and was eager to take his uniform off once and for all. He was hitchhiking with a heavy duffel bag. Flashing his thumb to an oncoming car, he lost hope when he saw that it was a shiny black limousine, so new that it had a temporary license in the back window—hardly the type of car that would stop for a hitchhiker.

But to his surprise, the car stopped and the passenger door opened. He ran toward the car, placed his duffel bag carefully in the back, and slid into the leather-covered front seat. The friendly smile of a handsome older gentleman with distinguished gray hair and a deep tan greeted him.

"Hello, son. Are you on leave, or are you going home for good?"

"I just got out of the Army, and I'm going home for the first time in several years," answered Roger.

"Well, you're in luck if you're going to Chicago." The man smiled.

"Not quite that far," said Roger, "but my home is on the way. Do you live there, mister?"

"The name's Hanover. Yes, I have a business there." And with that, they were on their way.

After giving each other brief life histories and talking about everything under the sun, Roger, who was a Christian, felt a strong compulsion to witness to Mr. Hanover about Christ. But witnessing to a wealthy businessperson who obviously had everything he could ever want was a scary prospect indeed. Roger kept putting it off, but as he neared his destination, he realized it was now or never.

"Mr. Hanover," began Roger, "I would like to talk to you about something very important." He then proceeded to explain the way of salvation, ultimately asking Mr. Hanover if he would like to receive Christ as his Saviour. To Roger's astonishment, the big car pulled over to the side of the road. For a moment Roger thought that Mr. Hanover was about to throw him out. Then a strange and wonderful thing happened. The older man bowed his head to the steering wheel and began to cry, affirming that he did, in fact, want to accept Christ into his heart. He thanked Roger for talking to him, saying, "This is the greatest thing that has ever happened to me." Then he dropped Roger off at his house and traveled on toward Chicago.

Five years went by, and Roger Simms married, had a child, and started a business of his own. One day while packing for a business trip to Chicago, he came across the gold-embossed business card that Mr. Hanover had given him years earlier.

Roger looked up Hanover Enterprises and found it in downtown Chicago in an imposing high-rise office building. The receptionist told him that it would be impossible to see Mr. Hanover, but that if he was an old friend, he would be able to see Mrs. Hanover. A little disappointed, he was led into a poshly decorated office where a woman in her 50s sat at a huge oak desk.

She extended her hand. "You knew my husband?"

Roger explained that Mr. Hanover had been kind enough to give him a ride back home.

A look of interest passed across her face. "Can you tell me what date that was?"

"Sure," said Roger. "It was May 7, five years ago, the day I was discharged from the Army."

"And did anything special happen on your ride . . . anything unusual?"

Roger hesitated, wondering if his witness had created some source of contention between the two that had resulted in their separation. But he felt the prompting of the Lord to be truthful. "Mrs. Hanover, your husband accepted the Lord into his heart that day. I explained the gospel message to him, and he pulled to the side of the road and wept, and then chose to pray a prayer of salvation."

Suddenly she began to sob uncontrollably. After several minutes she regained enough control to explain what had happened. "I grew up in a Christian home, but my husband did not. I had prayed for my husband's salvation for many years, and I believed God would save him. But just after he let you out of his car, on May 7, he passed away in a horrible head-on collision. He never arrived home. I thought God had not kept His promise, and I stopped living for the Lord five years ago because I blamed Him for not keeping His word."

Never give up. God has ways. . . .

CHAPTER 10

Breaking Down Spiritual Strongholds

C hristian churches need to fight more. If your church is like most churches, then it probably does not have enough pugnacity in it. You may think there is already too much fighting in the church, but the truth is, we have too little, and what we have is usually directed against the wrong target.

The first few words of Ephesians 6:12 sum up the sad state of the church: "For we wrestle not" (KJV). That's the problem. But there is more to this passage, and it sheds a lot of light on what is going on in the invisible realms around us. Let's take a look:

"Put on the full armor of God so that you can take your stand against the devil's schemes. For our struggle is not against flesh and blood, but against the rulers, against the authorities, against the powers of this dark world and against the spiritual forces of evil in the heavenly realms. Therefore put on the full armor of God, so that when the day of evil comes, you may be able to stand your ground" (verses 11-13).

Paul goes on to list the spiritual armor that a Christian should be wearing, such as the breastplate of truth, the helmet of salvation, the shield of faith, and so forth. After listing each part of the defensive armor of the Christian, Paul stops talking in metaphors and gets down to reality: "Pray in the Spirit on all occasions with all kinds of prayers and requests. With this in mind, be alert and always keep on praying for all the saints" (verse 18). There's the weapon—prayer.

Tim was once preaching on this passage to a Filipino congregation in Glendale, California. They had chosen this text as their focus for a day of prayer and fasting in preparation for an upcoming evangelistic campaign. This was the second time they had done this. A few years earlier, they told Tim, they had gone for 24 hours without food to implore God to give them a new church. At the time they had no idea where their new church was coming from. Just one month later they met to worship in their new building, one that had suddenly come on the market.

It pays to wrestle with God.

According to Ephesians 6, our wrestling partners are not flesh and blood. In other words, our enemy is not any human being. Let's do a little experiment. Think of your worst enemy right now. Think of someone who makes your life miserable or has done you wrong. Maybe you'd like to get your hands on that person and (grrrr!) shake them up a little. Or worse.

But wait! That person is not your real enemy. He or she is only a decoy. Your real enemy is a being who is far more evil, far more intelligent, and far more powerful, and he's merely using this human being to get to you. Both you and the person you dislike are really only victims of the supernatural powers of darkness, the invisible forces of evil.

So if you're going to fight, don't fight with the poor soul whom Satan is using to get at you. Don't aim your weapons at the decoy. And don't employ obsolete weapons. Keep in mind that in order to fight supernatural beings, we have to use supernatural weapons. That's why the Bible tells us to pray for our enemies; pray for those who don't treat us right. Because every prayer strikes a blow to the heart of the evil one.

So next time you think someone's out to get you, remember that things are not as they seem. Your enemy is not human. If we would only wrestle in prayer *for* one another, we wouldn't need to wrestle *with* one another.

Paul mentions Epaphras, one of his coworkers, in Colossians 4:12. The apostle tells the Colossians that "he is always wrestling in prayer for you, that you may stand firm in all the will of God." We've got to learn to look beyond flesh and blood beings to the forces influencing them.

Jan was a bright, cocky, young male student attending a Christian college who was determined to break all the rules. And he pretty well succeeded. One of the rules forbade drinking. Jan broke that one, too. One day one of his more spiritual friends decided to try to persuade Jan to stop drinking. The two students got into a long and elaborate argument about the pros and cons of the matter, and, well, Jan won the argument. Jan was a very sharp fellow. Finally it got late, so they parted and each went to their respective rooms in the dormitory, with Jan as cocky as ever and his friend greatly concerned about him.

That night Jan couldn't sleep. He tossed and he turned, turned and tossed, and in his mind he went over all the arguments for and against drinking. Finally about 3:00 in the morning Jan decided that his friend was right; he would stop drinking.

The next morning he went to tell his friend the good news. He knocked, and his friend came to the door, looking rather bedraggled. "Guess what?" Jan began. "You were right. Drinking is stupid. I've decided to quit. . . . Say, how come you're still wearing the same clothes you were wearing last night?"

"Well, Jan," said his friend, "I've been up all night praying for you."

Now, this young man could have argued until he was blue in the face and still not persuaded Jan to give up that destructive habit. So he wisely decided to stop wrestling with flesh and blood and start wrestling with God. Today Jan Haluska is a professor of English literature at Southern

Adventist University, near Chattanooga, Tennessee, all because someone cared enough to pray.

~

We are blissfully unaware of the spiritual forces that we are really up against. Satan keeps us lulled to sleep so we won't use our weapons against him. He knows how powerful those weapons are, even if we don't! Meanwhile, the forces of evil are on the march.

Peter Wagner, in his book *Prayer Shield*, tells the story of a fascinating encounter on an airplane with one of the enemy forces. John Vaughan is a Baptist pastor, a university professor, and the editor of the *Journal of the North American Society for Church Growth*. He was flying from Detroit to Boston to do a pastors' seminar. On the plane he noticed his seatmate bow his head and move his lips as if praying. When he finished, John said, "Are you a Christian?"

The man seemed shocked by the question and said, "Oh, no. You have me all wrong. I'm not a Christian. Actually, I'm a satanist!"

When John asked him what he was praying for as a satanist, the other man said, "Do you really want to know?"

John said yes. "My primary attention is directed toward the fall of Christian pastors and their families living in New England," the satanist replied. Then he asked John what he was going to do in Boston.

After John told him about his ministry for the kingdom of God, the satanist indicated that he needed to return to his work!

Bill McRae, chancellor of Ontario Theological Seminary, was pastoring in London when he discovered that a group of satanists there had committed themselves to pray to Satan for the elimination of a number of evangelical leaders in the city. That year five Christian leaders fell through immorality and marital breakdown.

Never forget this: *we are at war*. And in time of war it is important to know who the enemy is, and it is vital to know our weapons. Often we think of prayer as a defensive weapon, something to protect us from evil. And it's true that prayer does work this way. In Psalm 50:15 God says: "Call upon me in the day of trouble; I will deliver you, and you will honor me."

But prayer is not merely a defensive weapon. It's an offensive weapon. We have the most powerful weapon ever given to humanity to be used in ransacking the kingdom of darkness. Our weapons, says Paul, are not the weapons of the world. On the contrary, he says, our spiritual weapons have divine power to tear down spiritual strongholds (see 2 Cor. 10:4). No multimegaton bomb could touch the fortresses we're up against. We've got something far stronger—so strong that Christ told us that the gates of hell will not prevail against it (Matt. 16:18).

Most people take this to mean that the gates of hell are attacking the church but are unable to prevail. But gates do not attack. What the verse means is that the gates of hell will not be able to *withstand* the onslaught of God's church. It is the church that is the attacker—or is supposed to be. So with a promise like that, why aren't we fighting to rescue those caught in the kingdom of darkness and bring them into the light?

Or have we grown accustomed to the dark?

Daniel's prayer for understanding resulted in three weeks of warfare between the angel of light and the principality of darkness controlling the nation of Persia (Dan. 10:13). Ultimately Gabriel prevailed, perhaps in part because of Daniel's three weeks of fasting and prayer, which apparently involved abstinence from meat, rich foods, and so forth. Daniel's wrestling with God in fasting and prayer helped to determine the destiny of his nation and temporarily defeat the forces that opposed the rebuilding of Jerusalem. The kingdom of darkness cannot withstand persistant prayer for very long.

Here is a modern "gates-of-hell" story. In 1992 Tim held two crusades in Mindanao, in the Philippines. The Filipino laypersons, under the leadership of local pastors, visited in homes and gave Bible studies before the series started. God blessed in the baptism of 476 persons in one day near the end of the first crusade. The second crusade, in Valencia, near Mountain View College, followed two weeks of preliminary meetings under the leadership of Pastor Edwin Gulfan. Each night a health lecture by Dr. Indrasenai Wijenayake ("Dr. Indra") preceded the sermon. At the end of that third week a baptism had been scheduled on Saturday morning. We take the rest of the story directly from the diary that Tim kept on the trip:

"Also working with our team is Dr. Indrasenai Wijenayake ('Indra'), from the South Philippine Union Mission, a converted Hindu and a gracious man, a man of faith. . . . At the river where the baptism was to be held, Dr. Indra came early and found two huge bulldozers scraping gravel from the bottom of the river and making a horrible racket. He asked them if they would stop for a few hours while we had the baptism. They refused, saying they had a contract and had to get the work done. So Dr. Indra suggested that in that case he would pray that God would cause their machines to break down. He prayed. Shortly thereafter the bulldozers stopped, and mechanics were seen working on them. By the time we arrived, peace prevailed. Twenty-four ministers officiated at the baptism. The final baptismal total for the day was 408."

~

Storming hell does not usually involve praying against machines. More often it involves praying for people. Specific people.

Wesley Deuwel, in his book *Mighty Prevailing Prayer* (Zondervan, 1990), tells of a Christian woman, bedridden for 17 years, who had been praying in a general way for the salvation of people for years. One day a zealous layperson challenged her to write down the names of all the people in her hometown of Springfield, Illinois, that she would like to be saved, and to pray specifically for their salvation three times a day. She accepted the challenge and enlisted others to pray for her names. In time, every single one of the 57 people on her list received Christ as Saviour.

When Burton Maxwell pastored a Seventh-day Adventist church in southern California, he tried to implement something like this among the members of his congregation. He hit upon the plan of giving each member a little pocket-sized book in which to keep an active prayer list of five names. These thin booklets have one page for each individual, with space for various facts about that person. Pastor Maxwell discovered that every 18 months, on the average, he would baptize one person out of each five.

Loren Nelson was called to pastor in Cottage Grove, Oregon, in 1973, after interning under Burton Maxwell. He believed in the power of prayer, and so he asked his members to list for him all of their friends whom they would like to see baptized so he could put them on his personal prayer list. The only condition was that the members had to be willing to go with the pastor to the homes of these individuals and introduce them to him. Loren ended up with a list of 86 names and set about visiting and praying.

Three years later Loren was called to a new district. Just before he left, he focused his attention on the very first name on his list. The man had never been baptized. He discussed the matter with his head elder, who took it upon himself to stay up all night praying for this prospect. The following day that man made his decision, was baptized, and eventually became head elder of the Cottage Grove Seventh-day Adventist Church.

And what about the other 85 names on the list? Well, by then they were already full-fledged members. Loren Nelson's prayerful labor resulted in the baptism of 86 out of 86 names in three years!

~

What sort of promises did Loren Nelson claim to win those 86 souls to the Lord? We don't know. But let's look at one of the most powerful promises in Scripture. The intercessor's Excaliber, it appears in 1 John 5:14-16: "And this is the confidence which we have before Him, that, if we ask anything according to His will, He hears us. And if we know that He hears us in whatever we ask, we know that we have the requests which we have asked from Him" (NASB).

Think about that! A blank check, as it were, from heaven's bank! And then John gives the application. He is not talking about praying for Lexuses, but for people. "If anyone sees his brother committing a sin not leading to death, he shall ask and God will for him give life to those who commit sin not leading to death" (verse 16, NASB). What a powerful promise!

Now, it's true that the offer holds only within certain limits. We cannot obtain forgiveness for "sin unto death," the unpardonable sin against the Holy Spirit. But within that limitation, we can actually confess the sins of someone else who does not care enough to pray for themselves and obtain forgiveness for that person.

When Israel rebelled, Moses asked God, "'Forgive the sin of these people, just as you have pardoned them from the time they left Egypt until now.' The Lord replied, 'I have forgiven them, as you asked'" (Num. 14:19, 20). Abraham interceded for Sodom (Gen. 18). Daniel prayed for forgiveness on behalf of Jerusalem (Dan. 9:15-19). Job offered sacrifices for the sins of his children (Job 1:5). Later Job had to intercede on behalf of his three friends before God would accept them (Job 42:7-10). James 5:15 says: "The prayer offered in faith will make the sick person well; the Lord will raise him up. *If he has sinned, he will be forgiven.*" Here again we are told that third-party prayers can forgive sin. "Therefore," James continues, "confess your sins to each other and pray for each so that you may be healed" (verse 16). God has given us intercessory authority to save souls for His kingdom.

Roger Morneau provides us with an amazing example of how asking forgiveness for a third party can work in real life. One day several years ago he parked at a store and rolled down the windows of his car to let the heat out. A few minutes later a green Mercury pulled into a parking place two spaces away. In the car sat a middle-aged couple; the woman was driving.

"Mary, you'll have to turn the key so I can roll up this power window," the man said.

"Jim, you're so stupid," replied the woman. "I've told you a hundred times to roll the windows up while the engine is still running. Won't you ever learn?"

The man burst forth with a flurry of profanities. Growing angrier by the moment, he accused her of wrecking a perfect day by refusing to keep her mouth shut.

Roger Morneau was thinking, *What a wicked man!* And then on a sudden impulse he prayed, "Jesus, please forgive them. By the mighty power of Thy Holy Spirit, please rebuke the demonic forces oppressing their minds and bless their lives with the sweet peace of Thy love."

Instantly the verbal storm stopped. For about 20 seconds neither said a word. Then the man broke the silence. "Mary, I am sorry I got so angry. Really, I feel bad now that I spoke to you in the way I did. I don't know why I get so angry at times. I can actually feel anger swell up in me toward people I dearly love. Please forgive me, and I promise to put forth real effort not to repeat these outbursts."

Then the woman admitted she was at least partly at fault for not being careful with her words. She acknowledged that she sometimes actually took pleasure in verbally jabbing him. Promising to be more considerate in the future, she gave him a peck of a kiss and put the window up. Then they both got out of the car to go shopping.

Stepping to the parking meter, the husband studied his coins to feed the meter. Since he had no dimes or nickels, he turned to his wife and said, "Sugar pie, would you be kind enough to look in your purse for a dime?"

"How can I refuse to help when you are treating me as a lady? Do you realize, Jim, that you haven't called me your sugar pie since the kids were little?" After he put the coins in the meter, she grabbed him by the arm, and like two newly-weds they proceeded to do some shopping.

Meanwhile, Roger Morneau sat in his car in a state of shock. It was the first time he had ever asked the Lord to forgive someone. Having acted on a sudden impulse, he was amazed by how quickly the Lord worked. And apparently, all because of one unselfish intercessory prayer.

That was the first of many such experiences for Roger Morneau. He shares his experiences in *Incredible Answers to Prayer* and its several sequels, *More Incredible Answers to Prayer* and *When You Need Incredible Answers to Prayer*.

Sometimes God doesn't work so quickly. Josephine Cunnington Edwards prayed for her brother Bill for 50 years—and even got a small church involved in the act—before her prayer was finally answered in a remarkable way. Mary, Bill's wife, who had become a Christian years earlier, shared the details with Josephine.

One day Mary found Bill in tears. He explained, "I heard the door open behind me. I turned around, and . . . Oh, Mary, it was the Lord! I knew Him by the nail prints in His hands. No picture can ever portray the love in His eyes. He said, 'Bill, I have a special request I have to make of you. I have 50 years of prayer for you to answer for. Your parents went to their graves believing that they would never see you again in the kingdom. Bill, I would love to have a grand surprise for them when they get to heaven. Won't you give your life to Me so that I can present you to them there?'"

∽

Tim was ministering in Brazil in September 1992 when he experienced a remarkable answer to intercessory prayer. That month the Voice of Prophecy staff was holding large meetings all over Brazil, and 25,000 people were baptized as a result. On his trip over, Tim read an article on prayer that made the point that on our own we are like a cold piece of steel, with no magnetic attraction. But when a piece of steel is brought into contact with a magnet, the magnetism flows through it and the steel itself becomes attractive. So when we are in contact with God, we become magnetic and draw others to God.

The concept was so appealing that Tim purposed to put the theory to the test by faithfully spending an hour a day in prayer during his time in Brazil.

One day Tim called his wife, Carol, and she asked him to please pray for a certain minister, a mutual acquaintance, because he was discouraged and thinking of leaving the ministry. This was startling news because Bill (not his real name) had been a highly effective minister up until that time. Some years he had led the conference in baptisms.

So all the next week Tim prayed for Bill with more than usual diligence. "I suppose I prayed as earnestly for Bill as I have ever prayed for anyone," Tim says. At the time Tim was giving a series of sermons on prayer to a group of 800 students in southern Brazil. He prayed that God would pour out so many blessings on Bill, and that so many of his members would affirm and encourage him, that he would abandon his plans to leave the ministry.

Near the end of that week, as Tim was praying, an impression came to him: "Not only am I going to answer your prayers for Bill, but I am giving you the same gift you asked for him." And God did! All that week Tim received an outpouring of love from the students. They sent him gifts, they wrote him notes, and they sang songs for him. (Remember, meet God's needs, and He'll meet yours.)

The meetings ended on Saturday night with a baptism, and Tim went to bed early with a slight headache. He thought the adventure was over. But in the middle of the night, at 1:30 Sunday morning, the singing group at the college got dressed and came knocking on his door to serenade him with the song "Friends Are Friends Forever."

Unforgettable. And that was the end of the headache.

A few days later Tim called his wife and asked if she had heard anything about Bill. Yes, she had. Through a third party she learned that Bill had said something like this: "I can't believe what is happening to me. My wife has never been so wonderful and kind to me. And my members have been so supportive. I don't understand what is happening."

~

Intercessory prayer works. Besides your loved ones, whom is the Lord impressing you to pray for right now? Who needs your prayers? What about your spiritual leaders? your coworkers? people you eat with? people you buy things from? What about your doctor or other professional associate? What about that young single parent with children? that neighbor?

One person you need to pray for is your pastor. It may be that someone out there has targeted your pastor with the powers of darkness, seeking his downfall. Paul repeatedly asked his converts to pray for him (Rom. 15:31; Eph. 6:20; Col. 4:4; 2 Thess. 3:2). Surely your minister needs the shield of your prayers as much as Paul did.

Why was James the apostle killed by Herod, but Peter miraculously delivered from his clutches (Acts 12)? We can't be certain, but possibly the first martyrdom caught the Christians by surprise, before they had thought to pray. The next time, however, they were ready, and their united prayers secured Peter's release. Our leaders need our prayers.

Should you want a new minister, just start praying for the old one. God will baptize him with such power that some larger church will come along and take him off your hands. If you want to talk about your pastor, talk to God. Pray for him every day, not just once a week. He'll go on from strength to strength in the Lord. And your church will grow and prosper.

Friend, you have an incredibly powerful weapon. The gates of hell cannot withstand it. As a result of decisions you will make today about your prayer life, someone headed for destruction may now live forever. Your persistent prayers will wound the prince of darkness and bring life to the spiritually dead. Use your weapons!

CHAPTER 11

Praying Down the Fire

A rchimedes claimed that if he had a long enough lever and a big enough fulcrum, he could move the earth. Christians do, in fact, have such a lever. Prayer is the lever on God's fulcrum that moves the world.

In the two previous chapters we have discussed the topic of intercession for others. But it is not enough to pray for individuals. We must pray that God will send a revival and begin a movement of His Spirit that will result in mass conversions. For only a mighty movement of God's Spirit can turn back the apparently inexorable tide of evil sweeping over the world.

Have you ever flown a kite? It's not easy to get it started. First you find out which way the wind is blowing. Then you run and run and spend a lot of energy just to get it a few feet off the ground. But once the wind catches it, it can go ever so high, and all you have to do is stand there and hold it. The wind makes a lot of difference.

Maybe if the spiritual life is hard for us, perhaps it is because we have not yet learned how to catch the wind of the Spirit.

Have you ever been sailing? A sailboat has no source of power within it. What makes a sailboat go? Wind fills the sails and pushes the boat along.

Now, what would you think of a man who took his sail-boat out with the sails furled and stowed away and started paddling around in it? He would be doing a lot of unnecessary work, wouldn't he?

Maybe we have been wasting a lot of time paddling the boat when all we need to do is trim the sails to catch the divine wind.

That doesn't mean that there is no work involved. Some people still remember the America's Cup yacht races in the late eighties when Captain Dennis Conner recaptured the title from the Australians. If you were watching that race on television, do you remember what the sailors were doing? Were they sitting back and enjoying the ride? Of course not. They were straining every muscle! But how? Were they paddling the boat and supplying the power? Of course not. The power was all around them. All they had to do was set the sails to catch it. They were furiously manipulating the sails to best catch the wind.

That sail represents prayer. When we pray, we are putting up the sails.

The wind of the Spirit moves in mysterious ways. Sometimes the ship of faith lies dead in the water—the Spirit isn't moving it. Then an unexpected breeze ripples over the waves. God has His seasons. The Spirit is sovereign and moves at unexpected times. But He usually moves in response to united prayer. God's whirlwinds are not planned up or organized up or preached up—they are prayed down. This has been well documented in recent decades by revival historians J. Edwin Orr and Wesley Duewel. Much of what follows is drawn from Orr's address to the 1976 Dallas Prayer Conference in Dallas, Texas, and from Duewel's *Revival Fire* (Zondervan, 1995).

In September 1857 a 46-year-old praying businessperson by the name of Jeremiah Lamphier decided to start a prayer meeting in the upper room of the consistory building of the North Dutch Reformed Church in Manhattan. He advertised his prayer meeting with handbills. On the day appointed he found himself praying alone. But by the end of the hour six people had shown up. The following week the group grew to 14, then 23. Soon they decided to meet every day for prayer. They filled the Dutch Reformed church, then the Methodist church on John Street, then Trinity Episcopal Church at the corner of Wall Street and Broadway.

By February of 1858 prayer groups crowded every church and every public building in downtown New York, and prayer meetings had begun to spring up all across America. Horace Greeley, the famous editor, sent a reporter with a horse and buggy racing around to prayer meetings to see how many men were praying. In one hour he could get to only 12 meetings, but he counted 6,100 men.

The revival had little or nothing to do with preaching. People gathered to pray. Sinners came to ask for prayer and were converted on the spot. Parents requested prayer for their unsaved children, and in a few weeks they would receive letters from them telling of changed lives. There were 10,000 conversions a week in New York City. The movement spread throughout New England. Church bells would summon people to prayer at 8:00 in the morning, 12:00 noon, and 6:00 in the evening.

The palpable presence of God seemed to hang over the land, and this canopy of grace even extended out over the Eastern seaboard. Ships approaching the East Coast began to feel its influence while they were still a hundred miles offshore. Ship after ship arrived, with the passengers telling the same story: passengers and crew had been seized with a conviction of sin and had turned to Christ before reaching port.

During this period churches could not baptize members fast enough. Trinity Episcopal Church in Chicago had 121 members in 1857. By 1860 the number had increased to 1,400. Many churches had a similar experience. Between 1 and 2 million people were converted to God out of a population of 30 million in one year. The revival jumped the Atlantic and broke out in Northern Ireland, Scotland, Wales,

England, South Africa, and southern India. It was a revival that began and ended with prayer.

When the revival reached Chicago, a young shoe salesman went to the Plymouth Congregational Church and asked if he might teach Sunday school. The superintendent said, "I'm sorry, young man, I have 16 teachers too many, but I'll put you on the waiting list."

"I want to do something now," the salesman persisted.

"Well, start a class."

"How do I start a class?"

"Get some boys off the street. Don't bring them here—take them out into the country. After a month you'll have control of them. Bring them here, and that will be your class."

The young man gathered a ragtag group on a beach on Lake Michigan and taught them Bible verses and Bible games, and then he took them to the Plymouth Congregational Church. Their teacher was Dwight Lyman Moody, and that was the beginning of a ministry that lasted 40 years.

To give you an idea of the nature of his first converts, here are their names: Madden the Butcher, Red Eye, Rag Breeches, Cadet, Black Stove Pipe, Old Man, Darby the Cobbler, Jackie Candles, Smikes, Butcher Lilray, Greenhorn, Indian, Gilberic. Moody's Sunday school class grew so large that President-elect Abraham Lincoln came to visit it.

Now, let's skip over a few years and look at one incident from the later life of D. L. Moody, as told by E. M. Bounds. Moody was taking a sabbatical in London for several months while his new church was under construction in Chicago. He had determined not to do any speaking, but one pastor prevailed upon him to speak at his church. After he preached that Sunday morning, he greatly regretted having promised to preach also that night. Later he said he had never had such a hard time preaching anywhere in his life. The church was absolutely cold and dead, without a trace of the moving of God's Spirit.

That evening, however, everything was different. The

church was packed, and the place was warm and alive with the Spirit. Moody said, "The powers of an unseen world seem to have fallen upon the audience." He was impressed to make an altar call, contrary to his plans, and 500 came forward. He sent them back to their seats, thinking they had misunderstood. He told them to count the cost, then made the call again. The same group came forward again. A major revival started in that church and that neighborhood. Hundreds of lives were changed.

What made the difference that night? It turned out that one of the church members had gone home from the morning service to where she lived with an old saint who could not get out to the service. When she told her invalid friend that they had a visiting speaker by the name of Dwight Moody, the old woman turned pale. "I read about him some time ago in the American paper, and I have been praying to God to send him to London and to our church. If I had known he was going to preach this morning, I would have eaten no breakfast and spent the whole time he was preaching in prayer for him. Now, sister, go out of the room, lock the door, send me no dinner; and no matter who comes, don't let them see me. I am going to spend the whole afternoon and evening in prayer."

And that was the secret of Moody's success there in London. Someone had prayed the price to break the ice.

By the way, D. L. Moody was instrumental in changing the life of F. B. Meyer, who helped to convert Wilbur Chapman, who converted Billy Sunday. The preaching of Billy Sunday brought transformation to a young man named J. L. Shuler, who later became a powerful evangelist in the Seventh-day Adventist Church. Another of Sunday's hundreds of thousands of converts was a man by the name of Mordecai Ham, and he brought a young fellow by the name of Billy Graham to the faith. And the story goes on.

~

Prayer doesn't work only in the West, it also works in the East. Let's talk about China.

In an earlier chapter we discussed Hudson Taylor, sometimes known as the father of modern missions, who devoted his life to China. After his death, a man by the name of D. E. Host took his place. Host wrote a book titled *Behind the Ranges,* in which he describes his attempt to analyze a problem he had seen while working in two different villages in China. The people with whom he lived and worked were not doing well spiritually. But those in the other village across the mountains were doing great! He visited them only now and then, but they were always doing fine, so he began to ask the Lord what was going on. How could those so far away be doing better than those with whom he lived and worked?

The Lord impressed Host that although he was spending much time counseling, preaching, and teaching those with whom he lived, he should spend much more time in prayer for the distant village. Host concluded that making disciples involved four basic elements: (1) prayer, (2) prayer, (3) prayer, and (4) the Word—in that order and in about that proportion.

Today China is once again burning with revival. The church is growing by leaps and bounds, publicly and in secret, and Chinese Communism appears to be doomed. The gates of hell are collapsing.

~

Tim is a keyboard artist. When he is asked to perform, if the piano is an upright, he will agree only reluctantly. There is little joy or satisfaction in plodding along on an upright. But on a well-tuned, fine quality grand, he can soar for hours without tiring. Not only is the sound quality richer, but the performance itself is superior because of the inspiring feedback.

God is like that too. He is the master of music; we are His instruments. We must allow Him to keep us in tune if we want to feel His fingers rippling over the keys of our lives in ways that feed others spiritually. God derives little joy from playing someone who, like sounding brass and tinkling cymbals, is out of tune. God can make music, if you plead with Him, on an old beat-up spinet. But oh, the surging power, the symphony of praise, when God finds a Steinway!

Evan J. Roberts was a Steinway.

How does one get to be a Steinway for God? Simply by wanting it badly enough to pay the price in prayer. All of his life Roberts had hungered to do more for Jesus. As a child he loved to pray and read his Bible. He went to church five nights a week. From the age of 13, as he worked in the coal mines, Roberts prayed that God would bring revival to Wales. Sometimes he skipped meals to pray, and he frequently rose in the middle of the night to plead for revival.

Please keep in mind that there can be no question of earning God's favor. The initiative lies not with human beings, but with God. God chooses an instrument and places within his or her heart a yearning for the salvation of others. But we can ask to be chosen.

At age 26 Roberts quit his job as a miner and became a student at Newcastle Amillennial College in training for the ministry. When Presbyterian evangelist Seth Joshua began revival meetings nearby in September 1904, he took Roberts and 20 other young people along with him. One day Joshua prayed, "Oh, Lord, bend us," and the Holy Spirit said to Roberts, "That is what you need." Roberts prayed, "Lord, bend me!" That day, after 13 years of prayer, Roberts received a powerful baptism of the Holy Spirit. From that moment he was ablaze for God.

Earlier we learned that we should not hesitate to ask a great king for great gifts. Roberts didn't. He pleaded with God for 100,000 souls, and God gave him the assurance that his prayers would be answered.

But how was God going to convert 100,000 souls, many of them rough Welsh miners? Well, evidently God decided to bring heaven down to Wales. God used other anointed servants besides Evan Roberts with unusual power during 1904. Throughout the country the citizens had an overwhelming sense of the tangible presence of God. He was everywhere—not just in churches, but in the streets, in homes, in the trains, in the mines. Even in taverns people came under conviction, leaving their drinks untouched on the counter.

Roberts felt impressed to get permission to leave his classes and return to his family to began a series of meetings in his hometown of Loughoron. He asked the pastor if he could speak to those present at a prayer meeting. Somewhat reluctantly the pastor allowed him to speak to those who cared to wait to hear him *after* the meeting. Seventeen people stayed to hear him.

"I have a message for you from God," Roberts said. "You must confess any known sin to God and put right any wrong done to someone else. Second, you must put any doubtful habit out of your life. Third, you must obey the Spirit promptly. And finally, you must confess your faith in Christ publicly." The meeting was a difficult one, but by 10:00 p.m. all 17 had responded.

The pastor, impressed, invited him back to preach on the following night, then for the entire week following.

During his meetings Roberts did little preaching. He would recite God's promises about the Holy Spirit. Then the Spirit led him to ask his congregation to pray out loud, one after another, "Send the Holy Spirit now, for Jesus' sake." Each night more individuals surrendered to the power of God. The meetings rapidly drew larger and larger crowds. Soon newspaper headlines read: "Great crowds of people drawn to Loughoron." One article said that a young man by the name of Evan Roberts was causing great surprise. The main road on which the church stood was packed with people trying to get in. Many closed their shops early to find a seat.

One reporter wrote that the meeting he attended closed at 4:25 in the morning, and then the people didn't seem to want to go home! They were still standing outside the church, talking about what had happened. In a very British summary, he wrote, "I felt this was no ordinary gathering."

Once the news media spotlighted the movement, it spread like wildfire across Wales. God kept His promise. One hundred thousand people were converted in the five months of that revival.

Roberts was once asked his secret. "I have no secret," he said. "Ask and ye shall receive."

Five years later J. V. Morgan wrote a book to debunk the revival. His main criticism was that of the 100,000 who had joined the churches during the revival, only 80,000 still stood firm. Only 80,000!

The cultural values of Wales changed overnight. Bookshops sold out of Bibles. The crime rate plummeted. Taverns went bankrupt. The illegitimate birth rate dropped 44 percent within a year. Drunkards and gamblers and broken families were healed.

The district counsels held emergency meetings to discuss what to do with the police, who had nothing to do. In fact, they sent for one police sergeant and asked, "What do you do with your time?"

"Well, before the revival we had two main jobs: one was to prevent crime, and the other was to control crowds, as at football games. But since the revival started, we have practically no crime, so now we just go with the crowds."

"What does that mean?" the official asked.

"Well," he said, "you know where the crowds are: they're packing the churches."

"How does that affect the police?"

"Well, among the 17 police in our station, we have three quartets, and if any church wants a quartet, they simply call the police station!"

A slowdown occurred in the mines. So many Welch coal miners were converted and stopped using bad language that the horses that pulled the carts in the mines couldn't understand what was being said to them. It took a while before the horses grew accustomed to the mild language.

The people spent their free time in revival meetings, up to four a day, at 7:30 a.m., 10:00 a.m., 2:00 p.m., and 7:00 p.m. The latter meetings often lasted until the early-morning hours. There was much spontaneous singing. When one church was full, the meetings would overflow to another church down the street. People would walk up and down the streets singing hymns, sometimes all night.

So great was the impact of that movement that revival swept Great Britain and broke out in Norway. It so moved Norway that the Norwegian parliament passed special legislation to permit laypersons to conduct Holy Communion because the clergy couldn't keep up with the number of converts who wanted to participate. The movement swept Sweden, Denmark, Germany, Canada, Australia, New Zealand, Africa, Brazil, Mexico, Chile, and of course, the United States.

Revival fire leaped over the Atlantic and broke out in America in 1905. Unfortunately, the Seventh-day Adventist Church was preoccupied at the time with the defections of Ballenger and Kellogg.

According to Kenneth Scott Latourette, one of the leaders of the 1905 revival, fully 25 percent of the student body at Yale University enrolled in prayer meetings and Bible studies that year. J. Edwin Orr mentions three cities as examples. The ministers of Atlantic City reported that out of a population of 50,000, only 50 adults were left unconverted. The pastor of the First Baptist Church of Padukah, Kentucky, was an old man by the name of J. J. Cheek. He took in 1,000 new members in two months and died of overwork. In Portland, Oregon, 200 department stores closed from 11:00 a.m. to 2:00 p.m. for prayer. They signed an agreement among themselves that they would not cheat and stay open.

Such a little spark can kindle such a great fire. Evan Roberts asked God for 100,000 souls, and after 13 years of prayer, he got them and more.

So what have you been asking God for lately?

~

We need a revival in our churches in the worst sort of way. But it has a price. The price of revival is prayer. It takes persistent, united prayer to bring a revival. God has promised, "If my people, who are called by my name, will humble themselves and pray and seek my face and turn from their wicked ways, then will I hear from heaven and will forgive their sin and will heal their land" (2 Chron. 7:14).

How would you like God to begin a revival in your church? Could God do for us what He did for Wales in 1904? Better yet, could He do for us what He did for Christians in the Roman Empire back in the days of Acts? Well, He could if we prayed like they did. The book of Acts has more references to prayer than any other book of the Bible. The very first one is quite succinct: "They all joined together constantly in prayer" (Acts 1:14). That's the condition. That's the price of revival.

In John 20:21 we find Jesus bestowing His Holy Spirit upon His disciples. Jesus says, "'As the Father has sent me, I am sending you.' And with that he breathed on them and said, 'Receive the Holy Spirit.'" This was a down payment on the fullness of the Spirit that would be poured out on the church at Pentecost. In the Old Testament only prophets, priests, and kings received the Holy Spirit. But in the gospel dispensation the Holy Spirit is poured out on sons and daughters; maids and milkmen; butchers, bakers, and candlestick makers. Common people like you and me. God says to each of us today, "As the Father sent Me, I am sending you." And He is waiting just now to waft His gentle breath into your soul as a down payment of the mighty tempest of power that is to come. Are you ready to receive it?

In Jeremiah 33:3 God says: "Call to me and I will answer you and tell you great and unsearchable things you do not know." Call on Me. I'm waiting. Turn off the television and dust off the family altar. Pray together with one purpose and one accord, and watch Me do things beyond imagining. Watch Me tap into My hidden treasure and unleash rivers of resources you never knew existed. Watch Me unbolt locked doors and tear down strongholds and batter down the gates of hell. Watch Me set the church on fire to burn vast swaths of enemy territory. Watch Me create a new future for your life and your congregation. Just call on Me. Seek My face. Here I am. Waiting.

Why not let your church be the beginning of God's next great revival. If you would like to see that happen, then just pray. One by one, two by two, in small groups, this week, next week, and next year, pray like you have never prayed before. Call a moratorium on theological nitpicking and pray without ceasing. Pray in season and out of season. Pray as if your life depended on it. Pray as if there were no tomorrow. Fast and pray until you hear the sound of abundant rain. Pray until God sends the mighty rushing wind. Pray until the fire falls. Just pray. And claim God's amazing promise in Matthew 21:22: "If you believe, you will receive whatever you ask for in prayer."

CHAPTER 12

How to Catch the Wind

In the previous chapter we discussed some of the great revivals in the past 200 years in the English-speaking world that came about as a result of prayer. But what about the Seventh-day Adventist Church? Have we not seen God's Spirit moving upon us as well?

Some modern Adventists would be appalled if they could travel back in time and observe one of our Adventist pioneers' early praise meetings. Here is how one of these pioneers described a meeting she attended in 1850: "Sunday the power of God came upon us like a mighty rushing wind. All arose upon their feet and praised God with a loud voice; it was something as it was when the foundation of the house of God was laid. The voice of weeping could not be told from the voice of shouting. It was a triumphant time; all were strengthened and refreshed. I never witnessed such a powerful time before" (*Manuscript Releases*, vol. 5, p. 226).

Sounds kind of fanatical, doesn't it? But those are the words of Ellen White. And in 1848 she wrote: "The power came down like a mighty, rushing wind, the room was filled with the glory of God, and I was swallowed up in the glory and taken off in vision" (*ibid.*, p. 249).

Now, that's quite a wind—one that hasn't been around in a while. But it has been here before.

In 1892 a remarkable revival began at Battle Creek College and spread out from there. It started this way. Two students at the college had gotten into trouble. One of them was an avowed unbeliever, the other had shown no signs of being a Christian. The faculty wondered what to do about their infraction, while at the same time they tried to establish an attitude of eager expectation for the upcoming Week of Prayer, something they didn't want to jeopardize. So several of the teachers prayed for and engaged in "personal labor" for the young men in trouble. Then on a Tuesday night, November 29, something remarkable happened. We quote Roy Graybill's account in *Insight,* March 30, 1971:

"The two young men . . . lived in different dormitories, but at almost the same time that evening, without having attended any meeting and without having consulted each other, both of them approached faculty members and, after telling of a severe struggle, gave their hearts to God.

"Then the whole campus began to move as if by some secret signal. That same evening other students left their rooms, deeply troubled, to seek counsel from teachers. Study hall was broken up by little groups meeting in various rooms to talk about their need of conversion, and soon the lobby was filled with students engaged in a praise meeting."

The revival spread to the offices of the Review and Herald Publishing Association. Uriah Smith described the revival this way:

"The Lord has graciously visited His people in Battle Creek during the past week. Especially has this been the case in the college and Review Office. This work was not the result of any particular efforts of a revival nature, but it seemed to spring up in places and in hearts where it was least expected. In the college the interest was so great that the regular studies were entirely suspended one entire day. Many were converted, some in the seclusion of their own rooms. In the [Review] office, meetings have been held in the early morning, at noon, and at night, with most blessed and happy results. Brethren who have been alienated from each other were made one in Christ, and sinners were converted to God" (Uriah Smith, in *Review and Herald*, Dec. 6, 1892).

Another reported: "Friends at a distance will be glad to learn of the good work being done at the college in Battle Creek, during the Week of Prayer just ending, December 24, 1892. Thursday and Friday were days long to be remembered by those who participated in these meetings for seeking God. As one remarked, 'It seemed as if a blessing hung over our heads ready to be poured out, but something hindered.' On Thursday the clouds broke, the spirit of confession took hold of teachers and pupils alike, and it was most heartfelt and genuine. Wrongs that were of long standing were confessed, and anguished hearts could no longer bear the burden that had prevented their full and free acceptance. Some had criticized their teachers, and had passed judgment upon everyone they knew or heard speak; others confessed to pride and selfishness of heart; many confessed unfaithfulness in schoolwork, and of breaking the rules, which they knew were good and wholesome. Some teachers said they had not sought God as they should before entering their classes, and with deep humility each one asked forgiveness of those who had been ill affected by his conduct or teaching" (Malcolm Bradley Duffie, in *Review and Herald*, Jan. 10, 1893).

When in Australia Ellen White heard the news, she was overjoyed. "I rejoiced when I heard that the Holy Ghost had been poured out upon our people in America, and I have been anxiously waiting new developments in America as was seen after the Holy Spirit descended on the day of Pentecost" (*Manuscript Releases*, vol. 5, p. 232).

Soon the revival spread to other areas, such as South Lancaster, Massachusetts. Ellen White describes a meeting there: "The glory of God came into that meeting. It seemed at times at the commencement of the meeting that the glory of God was about to drop upon us, but it did not come only to a few, but at this time like a tidal wave it swept through that congregation, and what a time of rejoicing" *(ibid.,* p. 234).

Like most revivals, this one no doubt had its occasional excesses and perhaps some unusual manifestations, and for the next few years Ellen White had quite a lot to say about fanaticism. But she directed most of her warnings, not against fanaticism, but against those who warned against fanaticism!

"He who charges the work of God to undue excitement, and calls it fanaticism," she wrote, "is certainly standing on dangerous ground" *(Review and Herald,* Feb. 13, 1894). "Should the Lord work upon men as He did on and after the day of Pentecost, many who now claim to believe the truth would know so very little of the operation of the Holy Spirit that they would cry, 'Beware of fanaticism.' They would say of those who were filled with the Spirit, 'These men are full of new wine.' . . . When souls long after Christ, and seek to become one with Him, then those who are content with the form of godliness exclaim, 'Be careful, do not go to extremes'" *(Selected Messages,* book 2, p. 57).

"There are some who are already questioning the work that was so good, and that should have been most highly appreciated. They are looking upon it as a certain species of fanaticism.

"It would be surprising if there were not some, who, not being well-balanced in mind, have spoken and acted indiscreetly; for whenever and wherever the Lord works in giving a genuine blessing, a counterfeit is also revealed, in order to make of none effect the true work of God. Therefore we need to be exceedingly careful. . . .

"But because some have misappropriated the rich blessing of heaven, shall others deny that Jesus, the Saviour of the world, has passed through our churches, and that to bless? . . . If this attitude is preserved, then when the Lord shall again let His light shine upon the people, they will turn from the heavenly illumination, saying, 'I felt the same in 1893, and some in whom I have had confidence said that the work was fanaticism.' Will not those who have received the rich grace of God, and who take the position that the working of the Holy Spirit was fanaticism, be ready to denounce the operations of the Spirit of God in the future?" *(ibid.,* book 1, pp. 141-143).

We should be cautious about automatically condemning extraordinary behavior at times when God's Spirit is working in a powerful way, for such behavior has attended some of the greatest revivals in history, including that of Acts 2. Still commenting on this revival, Ellen White wrote: "When the Holy Spirit works the human agent, it does not ask us in what way it shall operate. Often it moves in unexpected ways" *(Testimonies to Ministers,* p. 64). "The Comforter is to reveal himself, not in any specified, precise way that man may mark out, but in the order of God; in unexpected times and ways that will honor his own name" *(Ellen G. White 1888 Materials,* p. 1478; see also *Fundamentals of Christian Education,* p. 434; *Testimonies to Ministers,* p. 284). Sometimes God honors His name in strange ways. When proud individuals of culture and dignity, for example, end up grovelling on the ground in the presence of God, as has happened in many great revivals (such as those of Wesley and Whitefield), we have reason to suspect that something supernatural is happening. The Holy Spirit has done stranger things than this. On at least three different occasions in Bible times the Spirit prompted anointed leaders to strip down to their underwear (if not beyond) in public (1 Sam. 19:23, 24; 2 Sam. 6:14, 20; and Isa. 20:2-4).

Earlier in her life some suspected Ellen Harmon herself of fanaticism, because they could not accept some of the physical manifestations that attended her new and vibrant faith, such as prostration. Around 1843 one such opponent "who had confessed that he was wrong in his opposition experienced the power of God in so great a degree that his countenance shone with a heavenly light, and he fell helpless to the floor. When his strength returned, he again acknowledged that he had been ignorantly warring against the Spirit of the

Lord in cherishing the feeling he had against me. In another prayer meeting still another member of the same family was exercised in a similar manner and bore the same testimony. A few weeks after, while the large family of Brother P were engaged in prayer at their own house, the Spirit of God swept through the room and prostrated the kneeling suppliants. My father came in soon after, and found them all, both parents and children, helpless under the power of the Lord. Cold formality began to melt before the mighty influence of the Most High" (*Testimonies,* vol. 1, pp. 47, 48).

Since the 1840s such physical manifestations have cropped up infrequently among Adventists, and when they did, they were sometimes of dubious origin, calling forth Ellen White's rebuke (see *Selected Messages,* book 2, pp. 25-30; book 3, pp. 363-378). But the church has rarely been in danger of being overrun by exhuberant members afflicted with an excess of joy. We cannot help citing here one more poem by Elizabeth Rooney, who hails from the high church tradition. She titled it "Charismatic."

You're sure that it's all right to be ecstatic?
You're sure I have permission to be free?
You're sure they won't consider me erratic
If I am overcome by mystery?

I am afraid, Lord, scared to take a chance,
Afraid of ecstasy, afraid of You,
Afraid of love, afraid of radiance!
How can I keep the smiles from breaking through?

If I make music, Lord, or try to sing,
Or, worse, begin to dance,
You know it won't be quite the proper thing
And everyone will look at me askance.

When You dared love, they met You with the cross.
Dare I dare joy and count my life no loss?

~

In the fall of 1970 a major revival began at Andrews University and swept around the world in Adventist circles.

That year Andrews was seething with dissidence, drug abuse, and racial polarization. Hairstyles and dress were divisive issues on campus. The raucous crows of the 1960s had come to roost at Andrews.

Certain members of the faculty and a group of students began to pray for revival to come. Before school started they laid plans to have a fall Campus Concern Retreat at Camp Michiana involving the student leaders and others. The students who came had already been studying and praying together for at least a year. They were dedicated to changing the status quo.

Guest speakers for the retreat were E. L. Minchin, H.M.S. Richards, Jr., and a 29-year-old pastor by the name of Mike Stevenson. Stevenson was convinced that formalism, not fanaticism, was the problem in the Seventh-day Adventist Church.

What happened next illustrates a theme that runs through the revival literature: revival is more frequently sparked by testimony—often lay testimony—than by expository preaching (though we certainly need more of that). God calls men and women to be witnesses, not orators; channels of grace, not chalices of wisdom.

During the preliminary hymn singing at one of the main evening meetings, Stevenson felt deeply impressed that something out of the ordinary was about to happen, so he excused himself and went to his cabin to pray. When he came back he left his sermon notes behind and simply gave his personal testimony of what God had done in his life.

The result was an avalanche. The students began praying and confessing their sins at 9:00 p.m. and did not stop until 3:00 a.m. At one point they moved to a campfire and broke up into small groups and began to pray that the Lord would awaken those who had already gone to sleep, and many of them actually woke up out of a sound sleep, came to the campfire, and gave their hearts to Christ.

That was the beginning of something big.

When 150 spiritually revived students returned to campus they encountered skepticism and ridicule. But on Tuesday, at a 9:00 a.m. chapel, when they stood before the student body and told what God had done for them, it electrified the campus. The students invited their friends to give their lives to Christ. Chapel didn't let out until noon, and the school suspended classes that day. From there the revival just kept growing. There were all-night prayer meetings, chapel testimony services, and singing in the cafeteria food line.

The campus became polarized—some of the faculty were against the revival, some were for it. But the revival went forward, and hundreds of lives were definitely changed. The students had a bonfire in which they burned their drug paraphernalia, rock music albums, and pornography. The wind of God blew through the campus and cleansed it.

Immediately the Holy Spirit transformed the students into missionaries. Teams of youth went out to all the nearby academies and churches. According to the *Student Movement* of December 3, 1970, 18 students left the campus to carry the revival to Columbia Union College. The service at Sligo church, on the CUC campus, ran until 2:30 in the afternoon after an all-night Friday evening service.

Next carloads of students from CUC traveled at their own expense to surrounding churches to share the revival. Soon they hit Southern Missionary College (now Southern Adventist University), where 500 students volunteered to prepare a special Bible-in-the-Hand witnessing program. Over the next several years the spark ignited in the hearts of those Andrews students burst into flame and spread to many of the major Adventist colleges around the world.

～

Now, here is the curious thing. This didn't happen in a vacuum. The winds of revival swept over hundreds of college campuses that year. The first to be touched was Asbury College in February 1970. Asbury is a Wesleyan institution that had experienced major revivals in 1905, 1907, 1908, 1915, 1921, 1950, and 1958. Inscribed on the cornerstone of the campus church in which the revival began is a quotation from Hebrews 12:14: "Without holiness, no one will see the Lord."

On the morning of February 3, the students assembled in the campus church. Since there was no scheduled speaker, the new president of the college, Dennis Kinlaw, asked if any of the students had something they wanted to say. After a moment two or three stepped forward, and one of them began to talk.

Suddenly a powerful conviction settled upon the entire congregation, and students began streaming to the front. Others outside the church were spontaneously drawn inside. Lunch was forgotten in favor of confession of sin, reconciliation of enemies, and praise to the Lord. There was no leader. President Kinlaw sat down. Without any sort of leadership, that revival continued around the clock most of the week. Late Thursday night was the first time the auditorium was empty.

Why should it surprise us that God blesses other Christians who are seeking Him? Perhaps God wants to make us jealous and prod us to pray for the wind of His Spirit ourselves. At any rate, we must not make the mistake of the disciples who wanted to forbid someone from healing because he was not one of their group.

From the Asbury campus hundreds of students traveled all over the United States, bringing the revival to more than 200 other colleges. President Kinlaw explains what happened when they told their story in his book *Preaching in the Spirit:*

"Dr. Donald Irwin, pastor of the college church at Olivet Nazarene College in Kankakee, Illinois, was preparing to enter the Saturday night service of a weekend revival when his head usher told him two students from Asbury College wanted to see him. Noting that he still had ten minutes before the service was to begin, Dr. Irwin told the usher he could bring them in.

"Two very ordinary-looking young men strode into his

study. They told the pastor that revival had broken out at Asbury, that many people who had never known God were finding Him, and that Christians were finding Him in a more powerful way. These two fellows had been praying together the night before, when God told them they should visit Olivet College and share with the students what God was doing at Asbury.

"Dr. Irwin expressed his delight at the news, but indicated that he could not invite them to speak from the pulpit of the church because they were strangers to him. Their response surprised him. They said, 'No problem! God told us to come. We've obeyed Him. So everything's fine.' Dr. Irwin sensed no negative feelings on their part as he turned them away and they started down the hall.

"Dr. Irwin's own spirit checked him. He found himself calling, 'Wait a minute, fellows. Come back. How long will it take you to share your story? Could you do it in five minutes, after the first hymn?'

"They assured him they could do it in less time, if he desired. They just wanted to be obedient to the Holy Spirit.

"So after the opening hymn, Dr. Irwin briefly introduced the two students. The first stood and simply told who he was and how God was at work in Asbury College. He indicated that many people were finding God, torn relationships were being repaired, lives were being transformed, and the Lord had told them to come and share the news. He sat down, and the second student arose and said about the same thing. The two young men took no more than four minutes to tell their story, and there was no noticeable response from the crowd. Dr. Irwin announced that a quartet would sing next.

"The quartet finished their first verse. Before they could begin the second, their bass went to the altar, sobbing. Twelve to fifteen other people rose from various places in the auditorium and came to the altar.

"The service was being broadcast by radio. Many who listened felt the tug of God at their hearts, left what they were doing, and drove to the church. By nine o'clock there were more people in the sanctuary than when the service began. Many who came did not stop to take a seat but went directly to the altar to make their peace with God.

"The next morning, about twenty carloads of students drove from Olivet to churches and colleges around the country to tell about the revival. Wherever they went, the Spirit attended their witness as He had that of the two students the night before."

Someone did a little investigating at Asbury, and discovered that prior to the revival a small group of students had been earnestly praying that the Spirit of God would fall upon the campus. The prayers of that handful of earnest Christians unleashed a tornado of holy power that swept across America.

~

There is a simple pattern in most of these revivals. They began with prayer on the part of a small group of students or staff members. They did not begin with careful planning or inspirational music or even great preaching. They came through prayer.

All the Holy Spirit needs is an invitation and a channel through whom He can work.

You could be that channel.

Your prayers may have a far more powerful influence on the spiritual weather than you could ever imagine. Have you heard of the butterfly effect? Scientists have discovered that it is impossible, even in principle, to predict the weather very far ahead because something as small as the fluttering of a butterfly can affect it. Some butterfly could start a movement of air that could develop into a weather front.

So it is in the spiritual realm. Prayer is like butterfly wings. You could be the butterfly whose fragile prayer wings could touch off an avalanche of power and send God's whirlwind blowing through your community. Exciting, isn't it?

Maybe you are thinking, *My faith is too flimsy. I'm just a reed shaken by the wind.* Do you know what the wind can do with a reed once that reed lets go and surrenders itself to the wind? It's amazing! In a tornado something as insubstantial as air can actually drive something as flimsy as a straw *through the heart of an oak.*

The wind has the power to impart fear and remove fear. Several years ago an extremely strong windstorm swept through Ellijay, Georgia, where Tim was pastoring. Immediately afterward he was driving around town, surveying fallen wires and tree limbs, when he came upon two birds sitting in the middle of the road. Cautiously he drove toward them, expecting them to fly away any moment. They didn't. He pulled up right beside them, opened the door, picked them up, and set them on the front passenger seat of his car. The powerful winds had so dazed them that they had lost their fear of human beings. And when the winds of God's Spirit blow on us, it will alter our nature and we will lose our fear of what others are thinking.

Jesus once took 12 flimsy men and gave them three years of tutoring, with precious little to show for it. However, just before His ascension He turned to them and breathed on them, saying, "Receive the Holy Spirit" (John 20:22). When the Holy Spirit came, the fearful suddenly became brave, 12 blunderbusses became high-powered cannons for the Lord, and the world was changed. The same Holy Spirit is waiting today to do the same thing for us.

What does God have in store for His church for the future? Who will covenant to pray until God bends His Pentecostal jet stream to touch earth once again and wreak havoc on the kingdom of hell? What floods of grace is He waiting to pour out on your family, your school, your church, your town? Where will He find a channel through whom He can work?

The Spirit is drawing people by the tens of thousands, week after week, into His kingdom. More than one a minute join the Seventh-day Adventist Church. Yet that is only a trickle of what is to come. The 1970 revival was the last nationwide revival of this century. But once again something cataclysmic is in the air. The largest prayer meeting in

American history occurred in the fall of 1997 when more than 1 million men gathered to "stand in the gap" in the nation's capital. Prayer movements are sweeping the Adventist Church and many other churches. We are nearing home, and we are poised on the precipice of the greatest outpouring of God's Spirit that has ever been. Already we hear the sound of distant thunder. Soon those whose spiritual ears are tuned to God's frequency will hear the sound of a mighty rushing wind.

If your congregation or school is in need of the breath of God, then you know what to do. We can't control the wind. But we can pray. We can set the sails. We can be ready and waiting, sails unfurled, when the wind of God begins to blow.

Some of God's Greatest Promises

for answers to prayer Ps. 6:9; Matt. 7:7-11; Luke 18:27; John 15:7.

about His promises Num. 23:19; Joshua 23:14; Isa. 46:11; 55:11; 2 Cor. 1:20; Heb. 10:23, 35ff.

about miscellaneous needs Job 5:17-26; Ps. 34; 37:4; 81:10; 84:11; Mark 10:29ff.

for basic necessities Ps. 34:9ff.; 72:12; 145:15; Isa. 33:16; 41:17ff.; Matt. 6:25-33.

of God's love Ps. 103:8-17; Isa. 49:15ff.; Jer. 31:3; Rom. 5:8; 8:35-39; 1 John 3:1; 4:9-19.

for pardon Ps. 32:1-5; Isa. 1:18; 43:25; 55:7; Micah 7:18ff.; John 5:24; 6:37; 1 John 1:7, 9.

for assurance of salvation John 3:36; 5:24; Rom. 8:29-34; 10:9ff.; 1 John 5:9-12.

for victory over sin Eze. 36:25-27; Rom. 6:14; 1 Cor. 10:13; 15:57; 2 Cor. 5:17; Gal. 5:16; Phil. 1:6; 1 Thess. 5:23; Heb. 9:14; 13:22; James 4:7; 2 Peter 1:4; 1 John 5:4, 18; Jude 24.

for strength Ps. 18:32-36; 68:35; Isa. 40:28-31; 41:10; 2 Cor. 12:9; Phil. 4:13; Col. 1:11.

for healing Ex. 15:26; 23:25; Ps. 30:2ff.; 41:1-3; 103:2-5; 107:17-22; 118:17; Isa. 38; 58:8; Jer. 17:14; 30:17;

33:6; Mark 16:18; 2 Cor. 4:16-18; James 5:13-18.

for comfort in affliction Deut. 33:27; Ps. 34:18; 147:3; Matt. 5:4; John 14:18; 2 Cor. 1:3-7.

for relief from fear Ps. 4:8; 23:4; 46:1-3; 112:5-8; Prov. 3:24-26; Isa. 41:13ff.; 44:8.

for protection Deut. 33:12; Ps. 91; 27:1-5; 34:7, 19; 50:15; Isa. 43:2; Mark 16:18; Luke 10:19.

concerning enemies Ps. 21:11ff.; 118:6ff.; 138:7; Prov. 16:7; 20:22; Isa. 41:11ff.; Jer. 20:11.

concerning slander Job 5:21; Ps. 35; 31:20; 101:5; 120:2; Isa. 50:7; 54:17.

that justice will prevail Ps. 103:6; Isa. 42:1-4; Mal. 3:5; Luke 18:7ff.; 2 Thess. 1:6ff.

for freedom Ps. 107:10-16; 146:7; Isa. 51:14; 61:1; John 8:31-36; Rom. 6; 2 Cor. 3:17.

for peace Ps. 4:8; 119:165; Isa. 26:3; 32:17; Matt. 11:28-30; John 14:27; 16:33; Phil. 4:7.

for joy Ps. 16:11; 30:5; 64:10; 126:6; Isa. 30:29; 55:12; John 15:11; 16:22; 17:13.

for wisdom Ps. 111:10; 119:98ff.; 130; Prov. 2:3-11; Jer. 33:3; 1 Cor. 1:30; Eph. 1:17; James 1:5.

for guidance Ps. 23; 25:8-12; 32:8; Prov. 3:5; Isa. 30:21; John 7:17; 8:12; 1 John 2:27.

for success Deut. 28:13; 30:9ff.; Joshua 1:7-9; Ps. 1:3; 37:4-6; Prov. 3:1-10; Isa. 58; 48:15.

for recovery from failures and mistakes Ps. 37:23f; 116:6-9; 145:14; Prov. 24:16.

that good will come of evil Gen. 50:20; Rom. 8:28; 2 Cor. 4:16ff.; 12:9f.; 13:8.

that God will be with us Deut. 31:6, 8; Ps. 139:7-10; Isa. 41:10; Matt. 28:20; John 14:18, 23.

for the Holy Spirit Joel 2:28; Matt. 3:11; Luke 11:13; John 14:16f.; 15:26; 16:7-14.

to witness Ex. 4:12; Ps. 40:3; Isa. 50:4; Jer. 5:14; Luke 12:11f.; 21:12-15; Acts 1:8.

to soul winners Ps. 51:13; 126:6; Dan. 12:3; Matt. 4:19; 10:32; 1 Tim. 4:16; James 5:19, 20.

for successful intercession Job 42:8; Jer. 5:1; Joel 2:17-19; Rom. 8:26ff.; 1 John 5:16.

for your family Deut. 26:11; Ps. 89:30-34; 112:1-3; 115:14; 128; Prov. 14:26; 20:7; 22:6; 29:17; Isa. 49:18, 25; 54:13; Jer. 31:16ff.; Mal. 4:6; Acts 16:31; Rom. 15:5.

for backsliders Isa. 44:22; Jer. 3:12, 22; Eze. 18:21; Hosea 6:1; 14:4; Joel 2:12-14, 25.

for widows, divorcées, orphans Ps. 27:10; 68:5; 146:9; Isa. 54:4-8; Mark 10:29ff.

for the salvation of children Deut. 1:39; Ps. 102:28; 103:17; 112:2; Isa. 44:3-5; 49:25; 54:13; 59:21; 61:7-9; 65:23; Jer. 31:15-17.